ROMAN LAW AND THE LEGAL WORLD
OF THE ROMANS

In this book, Andrew M. Riggsby offers a survey of the main areas
of Roman law, both substantive and procedural, and how the legal
world interacted with the rest of Roman life. Emphasizing basic concepts, he recounts its historical development and focuses in particular
on the later Republic and the early centuries of the Roman Empire.
The volume is designed as an introductory work, with brief chapters
that will be accessible to college students with little knowledge of
legal matters or Roman antiquity. The text is also free of technical
language and Latin terminology. It can be used in courses on Roman
law, Roman history, and comparative law, but it will also serve as a
useful reference for more advanced students and scholars.

ANDREW M. RIGGSBY is professor of classics and of art and art history
at the University of Texas at Austin. He is the author of *Crime and
Community in Ciceronian Rome* and *Caesar in Gaul and Rome: War
in Words*, which received the Association of American Publishers
Professional Scholarly Publishing Division Award for Excellence in
Classics and Ancient History in 2006.

ROMAN LAW AND THE LEGAL WORLD OF THE ROMANS

ANDREW M. RIGGSBY

University of Texas at Austin

CAMBRIDGE
UNIVERSITY PRESS

CAMBRIDGE UNIVERSITY PRESS
Cambridge, New York, Melbourne, Madrid, Cape Town,
Singapore, São Paulo, Delhi, Mexico City

Cambridge University Press
32 Avenue of the Americas, New York, NY 10013-2473, USA

www.cambridge.org
Information on this title: www.cambridge.org/9780521687119

First published 2010
Reprinted 2012

A catalog record for this publication is available from the British Library.

Library of Congress Cataloging in Publication Data
Riggsby, Andrew M.
Roman law and the legal world of the Romans / Andrew M. Riggsby.
    p. cm.
Includes bibliographical references and index.
ISBN 978-0-521-86751-1 (hardback)
1. Roman law – Social aspects. I. Title.
KJA147.R544   2010
340.5´4 – dc22   2010018287

ISBN 978-0-521-86751-1 Hardback
ISBN 978-0-521-68711-9 Paperback

Lisae

CONTENTS

❀❀❀❀❀❀❀

ROMAN LAW AND THE LEGAL WORLD
OF THE ROMANS

1. INTRODUCTION

✧✦✧✦✧✦✧✦✧

ROMANS AND ROMAN LAW

Lawyer joke 1:

Q: Why don't sharks eat lawyers?

A: Professional courtesy.

Lawyer joke 2:

Q: How many lawyers does it take to screw in a light bulb?

A: None. They'd rather keep their clients in the dark.

Today the ancient Romans are probably best known for the dramatic and bloody parts of their world (say, gladiators and legions) or for the quaint details (think aristocrats wearing togas and carried in sedan chairs). But if we ask what their most important or most lasting mark on the world was, the answer would almost certainly be their legal system. Of course, many other ancient societies had legal codes, some long before the Romans'. A famous inscription now housed in Paris gives us the Code of Hammurabi, a set of nearly 300 legal rules from eighteenth-century B.C. Babylon. The five Old Testament books of the Torah offer us much Jewish law from rather later. The other great "classical" civilization, that of Greek Athens, has left us a substantial legacy of courtroom oratory. Yet over the course of centuries, the Romans developed something genuinely different. Their legal system was vastly larger, more encompassing, more systematic, and more general than anything else that existed at the time. Moreover (and through different routes) it returned to life even after the fall of the Roman Empire. The written remains of Roman law became the fundamental source for the so-called civil law that governs most European countries, and it has had a significant (if less direct) effect on the "common law" of England and the United States. These kinds of facts, combined with a certain amount of prejudice, have come together as parts of a common stereotype of the two classical Mediterranean civilizations: the Greeks were artists, thinkers, and writers; Romans were more practical people: soldiers, engineers, and lawyers.

Like many such grand generalizations, this one contains a small kernel of truth, but that should not distract us, especially when we want to look at the world experienced by individual Romans. *They* didn't organize their entire lives to be the sober, methodical ones in contrast to the more creative Greeks for our convenience. In fact, their attitudes toward the law were more complicated than the sketch I've just given might suggest, and in some respects were surprisingly modern. To get a clear view of this, we could do worse than to look at two texts written in the middle of the first century B.C. by the same person, but from two very different points of view. The person is Marcus Tullius Cicero, a politician, orator, and amateur expert on the law, and he will reappear throughout this book. The first text is a eulogy he delivered in 43 B.C. for the even greater legal expert Servius Sulpicius Rufus. It reads in part:

> He always approached matters arising from the laws and legal principles by appealing to convenience and fairness. He never thought it better to stir up lawsuits than settle disagreements.

The law is a noble, honorable calling. It settles disputes rather than creating them, and in general makes life better. Servius is the opposite of the lawyer as "shark" in the first joke just quoted.

The second is a bit of a speech delivered in late 63 B.C. At that time, Cicero was one of the two "consuls" (chief executives of the Roman government), but he was simultaneously acting as an advocate for a man who was on trial for (allegedly) using bribery in the election to succeed Cicero in office. Cicero argued (among other things) that his client didn't need to bribe anyone since he was obviously going to win anyway – the defendant was a war hero, while his opponent was a lawyer. While parts of the speech have a serious tone, this part works by using humor, and humor of a type more than a little familiar today. Cicero's weapon of choice is, in so many words, the lawyer joke. His point is not that lawyers are vicious (as in the shark joke), but that they obscure the issues behind clouds of artificial detail and complexity (as with the lightbulb example):

> It could be so easy. "The Sabine farm is mine." "No, it's mine." Then the trial could begin. But the lawyers won't

3

allow it. They say "The farm which is in the territory which is called 'Sabine.'" Plenty of words already, but they're not done yet. "I affirm that it is mine in accord with the law of the Roman people."

From there he goes on to play out all the technical moves and responses required to actually bring a case to trial. Imagine a modern document full of legal phrases like "party of the first part" and "collateral estoppal"; this is the Roman version. In one sense, Cicero's mockery is fair. Most of the legal language he quotes is well attested in reality (see [20] for the roundabout way of naming a piece of property). But it is less clear that the bits of legalese he has made up are *just* a wordier translation of the simple Latin he started with. In the real world, and especially in trials in which the other side may try to pick apart the language being used, those "extra" words may actually be necessary for clarity and precision.

For precisely the reasons many admire Roman law today, it generated a certain amount of suspicion in its own day. Its scope and sophistication made it the territory of experts. Ordinary people might not have objections to any particular law or regulation, but they could feel that the whole system was just a little beyond their control. There were similar objections to rhetoric in the ancient world. On the one hand, the art of public speaking was extremely important in a world without modern mass media. On the other, it involved special skills not available to most people. In either case (law, rhetoric), there was a system that was designed to achieve ends like justice and dispute resolution, but those systems were elaborate enough to take on lives of their own. To the extent that the law (or rhetoric) had internal goals, those might conflict with the broader society's desire for justice, fairness, peace, and so on. You should keep this tension in mind as you read this book. We sometimes talk as if ancient Rome were a nation of lawyers. Not only was this not the case, but many Romans were actively suspicious of lawyers. But they did generally recognize the value of a working legal system, and at a minimum they recognized the state's ability to impose law on parts of their lives. In what follows I will spend a lot of time talking about law as a Roman lawyer might have, but I will try to keep in sight the fact that most users of the law were not legal professionals.

PURPOSES

This book is meant to introduce you to the basics of the legal world of the Romans. I use the phrase "legal world" to bring together a number of different things. On the one hand, it includes the law roughly as it was understood by the Romans themselves. This kind of "law" has been used and studied almost continuously from Roman times. What rights and responsibilities were assigned by the laws? What procedures could be used to enforce these substantive rules? How, somewhat more practically, should or could you act in various situations to take advantage of the law (or at least to make sure you weren't tripped up by it)? But on the other hand, I also want to take into account the various ways in which the law interacted with the rest of the social world. How could actual people get access to the legal system? How much difference did various kinds of individual identity (age, sex, nationality, economic class, social status, etc.) make in legal matters? What kinds of cultural and economic values did the law support or assume? How much voluntary cooperation did the legal system assume or receive from individuals? How did the lawmaking and law-enforcing processes fit into the government more broadly?

One of the most important and broadest of these questions about the interaction of Roman law with the rest of society will not get its own chapter. Much of our information on Roman law comes from legal experts (see Chapter 3 for details). At first sight this would seem to be a clear advantage. Why wouldn't we want information direct from the best authorities? But in fact this set of sources may distort our perspective. Suppose two neighbors were involved in a property dispute, and imagine that the "correct" resolution was clear to a Roman expert. This expert opinion still might not control the actual outcome for a variety of reasons. One or both parties might distrust legal or governmental institutions in general. (Lawyer jokes haven't changed much since the first century B.C.) The parties might avoid a specific process because they misunderstood their actual rights. Or they might feel that compromise with a long-term neighbor was more important than enforcing abstract rights. Even if they did go to court, bribes, political favors, or stubborn local traditions might override the theoretical "right" outcome. The lack of a chapter on the broad version of this topic does not mean that it is not important. The discussion is broken up for two reasons. One is that the question is too big. Some of the individual questions I have just raised will get their own chapters (like Chapter 8 on social inequality and the law), and others will come up in multiple chapters. The other reason to break up the topic is that the evidence is scattered. As already noted, much of our information is from Roman lawyers. To compare their view to "what really happened," we need to have some other source of information. This is often lacking, and it is hard to predict where it will appear. Thus we generally have to wait for particular points of comparison to come up in their individual contexts.

Roman law's recorded history as a living system spans over 1,000 years. Over that time it went from being the municipal ordinances of the city of Rome to being the principal code governing tens of millions of people living throughout the Mediterranean basin and beyond. As a living law it naturally changed considerably over that time. Those changes were accelerated by the political fact that Rome grew from a modest Italian city-state to a vast, culturally diverse empire. This book will focus on what historians would describe as the late Republic and the Principate and legal scholars sometimes call the formative or pre-classical and classical periods (roughly 133 B.C. to A.D. 235; see Chapter 2 for details). This is in part because this period has drawn the most historical attention generally, and in part because many of the most important legal developments had taken place by the end of that time. For the most part, however, I will try to avoid chronological complexities and state much of the law dogmatically unless there is some specific historical point to be made. This creates some danger of oversimplification, but I hope the increased clarity will be worth it.

STRUCTURE

The main body of the book consists of twenty substantive chapters. Roughly speaking, the first half of the book is on the broader context, while the later chapters mostly treat the law itself. The chapters are short and are designed to be as independent of each other as possible. That is, it should be possible to read them out of the order in which they are presented. However, Roman law does not naturally break down so easily, and no two topics are ever genuinely independent. For the sake of space and to avoid boring repetition, I have tried to explain each major idea only once. As a result, there are a number of cross-references in each chapter to help the reader find those explanations. For the same reasons, I have included a glossary. This glossary serves another purpose as well. As you would expect from a legal system, Roman law uses a lot of technical terminology. Naturally, this terminology is in Latin. (In fact, scholars today sometimes use Latin terms differently than the Romans did and occasionally even make up Latin of their own. I will not burden the reader with which is which.) To keep the main body of the book as readable as possible, I have generally tried to keep the use of these Latin terms to a minimum. However, the reader who wishes to refer to more advanced works may find it handy to have access to the technical terminology. Thus I have tried to lay it out simply and conveniently in one place. I have also supplied an annotated bibliography of a few of the most accessible works on Roman law.

The most important supplementary chapter is a collection of documentary sources with commentary. In part, these documents will help illustrate the general principles discussed in the main chapters by showing actual individual cases. They also help address the questions raised earlier about the relationship between theory and practice. The items selected for this chapter will all be keyed to issues raised in the main chapters, but they should also be legible in themselves. As a result, this chapter should give a cross-sectional view of Roman law.

While this book is not intended as a general introduction to law or to any non-Roman legal system, I have tried to introduce modern comparisons that may be useful to the reader. In some cases the parallel (or contrast) is helpful for clarification, for additional explanation of just what is going on in the Roman case. Elsewhere there are broader and more substantive considerations in play. Many legal rules (in any system) involve compromises between different values, like fairness versus efficiency versus certainty of getting the right answer or interests of the parties in court (say, divorcing parents) versus those of persons not represented (say, children or society at large). As a result, there will obviously be different solutions to similar legal problems, and the contrasts will be instructive about Roman society more generally. Since the audience for this book is English-speaking, the modern system (or family of systems) most referred to will be the "common law," which arose in England and forms the basis for much of the law of the United States and other former British possessions. Keep in mind, however, that common law systems can differ from each other on individual points, and I have introduced only enough information to make points about Rome. Do not expect practical legal advice here!

In light of contemporary concern for sexist language, I have made an effort to vary the gender of pronouns referring to indefinite persons. It should be noted, however, that the society being described was a very male-dominated one, and so many (mostly masculine) pronouns should be understood to have their literal force.

I would like to thank several people for extremely helpful comments on drafts of this book: Lisa Sandberg, Michael Alexander, and Tom McGinn; Russell Hahn for his professional copy editing; and Beatrice Rehl for the idea.

2. ROMAN HISTORY – THE BRIEF VERSION

ROMAN HISTORY IS usually divided into three periods based on the form of the central government: the "monarchy" or "regal period," when kings ruled; the "Republic," a more democratic government; and the "Empire," when (naturally) emperors ruled. (Note that Rome was an empire [small e] in the sense of "conquering power" centuries before emperors came to the throne. I will use the capitalized "Empire" to refer to the time and form of government.) These divisions are not necessarily as important for the legal system as they are for some other aspects of Roman life, but they do determine where law came from, and give a general background against which to set specifically legal developments. The first three sections of this chapter will give brief explanations of the forms of government that define these three periods. The fourth will mention a slightly different way of dividing things up that is more closely tied to legal history. The final one explains the history of a specific institution that is especially important for Roman law: Roman citizenship.

THE MONARCHY

Roman legend has it that the city was ruled by kings from its founding (in perhaps 753 BC) until a coup which removed not only the last king but the kingship altogether (in 509 BC). Modern scholarship finds these dates (especially the one for the founding) highly suspect, and questions how and even whether the individual events happened. Most historians today do not believe stories that attribute any particular act to any of the legendary kings. Nearly the only agreed-on truth about this period is that Rome was ruled by a series of kings in the early days. Fortunately, for our purposes, we do not need to resolve any of the more specific historical questions. I just want to give a general idea of what kind of government was putting laws into place. Still, even saying there was a "king" (Latin *rex*) is potentially misleading. These kings were not hereditary rulers. In fact, some of them seem not to have been born Romans at all. Instead, they were elected, sometimes by the populace, sometimes by a Senate, when the previous king died. Once in office, they seem to have acted as lawgivers (as well as generals, priests, judges, city planners), but their power was not unlimited in the manner of some later European monarchs. It has been suggested (though not proven) that the kings were *meant* to be relatively weak, serving more as arbiters between the other leading men than as real heads of government. The later Roman government featured a "Senate," which appears to go back to this earliest period. It seems to have been an advisory body for the king, rather than a legislature of the sort now suggested by the name.

Whether the topic is law, government, or nearly anything else, we are very poorly informed about Rome of the monarchical period. Our surviving written sources mostly come from about 500 years and more after the fact; this is nearly twice the time between the present day and the founding of the United States of America. We have a number of fragments of laws attributed to "kings," and even to particular ones of them. Some of these may actually be genuine. A couple, for instance, contain a penalty clause meaning something like "let him be dedicated to the gods." The same wording happens to appear in an otherwise hard-to-read law that survives from a rare inscription of the period on stone. Still, it is nearly impossible at this distance to tell which fragments are genuine, which are later inventions inspired by some bit of real historical information, and which are just pure fantasy.

THE REPUBLIC

In the standard Roman story, the kings were thrown out suddenly, and replaced by a pair of officials known as consuls. In theory, the consuls held most of the powers of the king, but in practice they were greatly limited because of the sharing of power between two men, because they had to get elected, and because they served only a year in office. (Reelection was quite rare.) They were chosen by the "people" (that is, the adult male

citizens). These same people got to vote on all legislation of lasting effect. The consuls' powers rested mainly on the ability to
issue temporary edicts and to propose legislation. Over the first
three centuries or so of the Republic, the details of this government evolved quite a bit, but the basic structure remained
largely unchanged. Other elected officials (collectively called
"magistrates") were created: praetors, aediles, quaestors, and
tribunes. (As with the consuls, so with the lower offices; more
than one person at a time held each post.) In principle, there
was a hierarchy of these magistrates, in the order just listed,
but the different offices also had specialized functions, so they
largely did not interfere with each other. For instance, the
various "praetors" could serve as generals and/or provincial
governors, but came increasingly to be in charge of the judicial system. "Aediles" supervised the markets and much of the
urban infrastructure. "Quaestors" served bureaucratic functions, often as the assistant to a particular higher magistrate.
"Tribunes of the people" were ombudsmen who protected
individual rights and, most importantly for present purposes,
were the main proposers of legislation. (The tribunes seem to
have originated as popular organizers and always remained a
little outside the hierarchy of the other offices.)

That legislation continued to be approved and the various
magistrates to be elected by the people. In principle, every adult
male citizen still got to vote on every question. But depending
on what was being voted on, there were different systems of
voting that made different people's votes count for more or less.
In the earliest days of the Republic, there was some struggle

over whether any citizen or just members of certain elite clans ("patricians") could hold office, but the broader view (also including "plebeians") won out by a little after 300 BC.

The Senate continued to exist during this period. By the end of the Republic, membership in the Senate was a more or less automatic benefit of being elected to one of the magistracies, and seats were held for life. While the formalization of these rules came fairly late, the general practice seems to have been customary as far back as we can see. Technically, the Senate remained a largely advisory body, now assisting the consuls rather than the king. Only the people, not the Senate, could pass laws. The Senate exercised power in two ways. Less importantly, laws were occasionally passed specifically authorizing the Senate to fulfill certain functions, such as choosing provincial governors. This was rare, and most of the instances are from quite late in the Republic. More importantly, political figures spent most of their careers in the Senate and very little in the magistracies. Hence, the magistrates tended to do as they were "advised" by the Senate. In particular, it became conventional (though never strictly required) to get legislation approved by the Senate before presenting it to the people for formal passage.

An important point about the Roman government that is probably not clear from the discussion so far has to do with its size. Two things make it almost unbelievably small from a modern point of view. First, we are accustomed today to government with many levels: not just cities and nations, but a variety of levels in between, such as counties, states, provinces, and ad hoc collections of any of these. Roman government was much flatter. Originally, Rome was a typical Mediterranean city-state. That is, the city plus its immediately surrounding territory comprised the whole "nation," so there was no difference between local and national government. As Rome's imperial territory grew, that original unified government was not much revised. It remained both the city government of Rome and that of the empire as a whole. As Rome absorbed other communities, it tended to swallow them whole, leaving their governments intact. This left a level of local government, but not as part of the Roman apparatus. Most importantly for present purposes, much of Roman law did not apply to them; they were left to their own local systems (see Chapter 21). And there was even less government at middle levels. Most conquered land was divided up into provinces, each with a Roman governor. The governor's main task, however, was to look out for Rome's interests (tax revenues, peace and stability), and even in these matters the real work was often outsourced to contractors called *publicani*. The governor's office was not really a general central government for the province (see further in Chapter 21). Moreover, Italy itself was not a province and did not even have a governor.

Roman government was also small because for the most part it lacked a permanent bureaucracy. A description of the American federal government might start out with the president, Congress, and the Supreme Court, but beneath these leading figures are something like two million employees (not even counting the military and the postal service), spread out over the whole country and arranged in multiple levels of hierarchy. The Republican Roman government, by contrast, seems to have had something like hundreds of employees in Rome and perhaps a few dozen in each of a number of provinces (again, not including the military; there was no state postal service). Additionally, most of these workers were so closely tied to one or the other of the elected magistrates that their power was probably even more limited than their small number would suggest. For instance, the major magistrates were attended by "lictors," a sort of honor guard armed (at least symbolically) with axes and rods. It has been suggested that these men could have served some kind of police function, but that seems unlikely, since they were only allowed to operate in the presence of the magistrate.

THE EMPIRE

For those who lived through it, the transition from Republic to Empire must have been a complicated and uneven process, dating from perhaps 49 BC (when Julius Caesar marched on Rome and seized power) to 31 (when his grand-nephew now known as Augustus emerged as the survivor of a series of civil wars), or perhaps even later if one wants to wait for all the formal features of the new order to come into being. Different players came, went, and changed sides over this period. And questions have been raised about how important legal formalisms were to the creation of that new order. This modern skepticism is justified by, among other things, the fact that the early emperors were hesitant to admit publicly that they were monarchs. For present purposes, however, we can avoid most of these difficulties. Compared to the period covered by this book (much less the whole scope of Roman history), the transition does not seem such a long one after all. And even if the emperor's power did not rest primarily on legalities, the effect of the new imperial system on the law is clearer.

Instead of creating a distinctive new government or even an office of "emperor," Augustus and his immediate successors left much of the Republican order in place, at least formally. One of the ways they changed its actual function was to hold many of its offices by themselves simultaneously. The emperor also controlled (directly or indirectly) the choice of most of the other officeholders. The assemblies were not immediately abolished, but they had ceased both legislative and electoral activities by roughly the end of Augustus' reign. The more subtle change was to transform most of the old offices into largely honorary positions and to move the actual power to other locations in the government. One new locus of authority, at least in the first century or two of the Empire, was the Senate. After hundreds of years as an advisory body, the Senate was given power to elect magistrates, pass binding laws, and even act as a court (at least for its own members). Of course, this "power" was in large part a formality. The emperors transferred these functions to the Senate presumably because a relatively small group of relatively well-known men was easier to control than the assemblies. In addition to the Senate, power came into the hands of a variety of new officials of various sorts, all answerable to the emperor. Some of the new positions were formally part of the emperor's household staff rather than of the government. For instance, since judicial appeals came to the emperor personally (see Chapter 4), his secretary in charge of petitions was a powerful person. Other new (or newly empowered) positions were recognized as part of the state: deputies (*legati*) who governed many of the provinces, a "prefect" in charge of the city of Rome, and a variety of other prefects, procurators, and curators. These men owed their positions to the emperor personally, and could be counted on to do his bidding.

The later history of the Imperial government (that is, of the third and fourth centuries and later) largely continued the same trends. Most of the Republican offices remained in place, although in purely honorific form, and the Senate also faded back into formal powerlessness. The old courts eventually disappeared, as the assemblies had earlier (for more detail, see Chapter 11). The fiction that the emperor was not a monarch faded, as did any distinction between his personal staff and the official government. There was also a steady growth in the number of and types of officials, even though the Roman government remained tiny by modern standards, perhaps reaching a few tens of thousands of civilian personnel.

From around 300, the eastern and western halves of the empire became increasingly separate; beginning in 395, the two always had separate capitals and independent emperors. In fact, even after the last emperor in Rome was deposed (in 476), there were self-described "Roman emperors" in Constantinople (modern Istanbul, Turkey) for almost another 1,000 years. This period is often described as "Byzantine" (the capital city had a third name – Byzantium). Justinian, whose central importance to Roman law we will see later, was one of those Byzantine emperors (ruled 527–565).

PERIODS OF LEGAL HISTORY

The threefold division of Roman history just described is fairly standard in political, social, and military contexts. Within it, the center of gravity has tended (rightly or wrongly) to be placed in the late Republic and early Empire. Students of the law, however, have tended toward a fourfold division and a somewhat later focus. The periods they choose have a double definition. On the one hand, they reflect changes in political authority – who is allowed to interpret the law – as power moves from priests to the so-called jurists (who were sort of like law professors; see Chapter 5) to the emperors. On the other hand, each period seems to have a different characteristic feel in terms of the law itself. How fast and how far does it change? How consistent and systematic is it?

This fourfold scheme begins with an archaic period, dating from the earliest days of Roman law to an ill-defined date somewhere in the third or second century BC This is followed by a late Republican "formative" or "pre-classical" phase lasting until the end of the (political) Republic and

perhaps a little beyond. This period is distinguished from
the archaic particularly by the rise of the "profession" of the
jurist. Republican jurists did show an increasing degree of
specialization and autonomy. Most of the important institutions of later Roman law had been developed by the end of
this period, but not necessarily systematized. A "classical"
period then ensued, lasting until roughly AD 235. In terms
of the legal profession, this period was marked by the growing absorption of legal expertise into the state. This process
began immediately with the empire, but worked out subtly
at first. In substance, this was a period of consolidation and
working out of detail. We see a series of writers producing
ever larger and more comprehensive works on the law until
the process comes to a fairly sudden halt with the fall of the
so-called Severan dynasty of emperors. It is probably no coin-
cidence that the end of this productive period coincides with
the beginning of several decades of relative political insta-
bility. What remains afterward is lumped together as "post-
classical," though this is hardly a unified category. In general,
we can perhaps say that this is a period in which the jurists
outside the government have lost most of their importance.
Instead, the important legal texts are enactments and codifi-
cations in the names of various emperors (though presumably
the actual authors are still legal professionals). The continuing
existence of texts from earlier periods created a conservative
if uneven force as well. In substance, then, the law of the
post-classical period does not take a particular direction of
its own.

ROMAN CITIZENSHIP

Ordinarily, in the ancient Mediterranean world, the basic political entity was the city and its surrounding territory. You were a citizen of, if anything, a city, like Rome or Athens, and typically this meant the city of your parents. There was relatively little geographical mobility, and citizenship did not normally take account of immigration. The growth of Rome into a large empire (in the sense of a conquering power) almost necessarily complicated this picture. Moreover, the Romans introduced some additional twists of their own.

In the days of the monarchy and early Republic, Rome was one of a number of communities in the west central Italian region of Latium that shared various features of religion, law, and language. (This is why people called "Romans" spoke a language called "Latin.") The residents of the various Latin cities retained formally independent citizenships, but the lines did blur somewhat. Latins could engage in marriages and commercial dealings in a way normally restricted to persons who shared the same citizenship. It was even possible to gain full rights in another Latin community (including voting rights) simply by moving there. As Rome grew stronger, the links among the other Latin communities were broken down, but each one remained individually tied to Rome (minus the right to move there). This made Latin status a kind of halfway version of Roman citizenship. At the same time, Rome was slowly conquering a number of other states throughout Italy. After their various military victories, the Romans organized their conquests in several different ways. In some places they seized at least part of the territory of the defeated state, declared it "Roman," and often eventually distributed it to their own people. In others, they left at least part of the defeated state in place, but placed it under treaty obligation to assist Rome in her future wars. And finally, they established entire new communities ("colonies"). Some of these were populated by Roman citizens, but many were declared to be "Latin." At this point, being Latin was no longer a linguistic (or ethnic or geographical) category, but a political one. That is, Rome took the package of legal rights and obligations that had previously distinguished the "real" Latins and started giving them out to others (even people who had been born Roman) as a matter of policy. Early in the first century BC many of the subordinate allies staged an uprising against the (by then greatly expanded) "Romans," while the Latins and certain other allies remained loyal. The Romans won a military victory, but in the process all communities on the Italian peninsula were decreed to be Roman.

During the time of the Republic, however, this spread of citizenship stayed almost entirely within the bounds of Italy. There were rare grants of citizenship to loyal foreigners (as a personal reward), and a select few colonies were established outside of Italy. This changed dramatically under the empire. First, colonies could no longer be established in the all-Roman Italy (which had come to include most of modern Italy by the mid first century BC). Thus subsequent placement of colonies (largely to settle retired veterans, rather than as the direct result of conquest) expanded the citizen-owned territory of

Rome. More importantly, beginning in the mid first century AD, various Roman emperors decreed citizenship for different groups of provincials. In many cases, this was done a city at a time; in others, the status of an entire province was changed at once. At least in some parts of the empire, there was an intermediate stage during which the once-foreign community was made to be Latin (a term that had now lost all connection to its local origins). The move toward a single citizenship was not uniform, but it went only in one direction. Finally, in AD 212, virtually all free inhabitants of the empire were made citizens by the emperor Caracalla.

3. SOURCES OF ROMAN LAW

✧✧✧✧✧✧✧✧✧

THIS CHAPTER IS entitled "Sources *of* Roman Law" in contrast to the next chapter on "Sources *for* Roman Law." The difference is that this chapter takes an ancient point of view. If you were an ancient Roman, where did the laws you had to live by come from? As the previous chapter noted, the Romans did not have a Congress or state legislatures or city councils to pass laws. Nor, for much of their history, did they have a king or other single dictator who could just issue decrees. How then were laws made? The next chapter will take up a modern perspective. How can we find out today what the law was then? Historians today must sort through often obscure, ambiguous, and contradictory evidence to answer almost any question about the ancient world. Where in particular do we need to look to find out about Roman law?

THE PRINCIPAL SOURCES OF LAW

Although Roman political institutions were different from those of the modern United States, the sources of law in both systems can be put into the same three general categories: "statute" law (law enacted by a legislative body), administrative rules, and judicial interpretation. This section will outline the Roman versions of these three types, noting changes in them tied to the transformations of the Roman government. I will point out similarities to and differences from modern practice. The next section will look at how the different sources interacted with each other.

Roman statute law during the Republic came from votes of the popular assemblies. The resulting laws were called generally *leges* (sing. *lex*); this is where our word "legal" comes from. (You may occasionally also see the term *plebis scita* [sing. *plebis scitum*], but the difference is only procedural; it does not affect the force of the law.) Unlike the American system, though more like the British, there was no separate Constitution or other kind of special super-law. The rules of government could in theory be changed by the same majority vote it would take to build public works, change tax rates, or increase the penalty for some crime. Rome's first written legal code was a collection of *leges* called collectively the Twelve Tables, dating to about 450 BC. Many of these laws remained on the books, at least formally, through the whole history of Rome. Under the Empire, some laws were still passed by the assemblies (though always with the approval of the emperor), but increasingly the emperor came to rule by issuing orders. As in the Republic, these laws could take on somewhat different names depending on the precise way in which they were created, but all just amounted to imperial decrees: "constitutions" (just an imperial order, not to be confused with a modern Constitution), decrees of the Senate (*senatus consulta* [sing. *consultum*] – recall that the Senate of the Republic could *not* make laws), and "responses" to individual appeals and petitions were all ways of enacting the emperor's will (though the details were presumably the work of professionals on his staff).

There had been rule by executive order even during the Republic. These decrees came not from bureaucratic agencies, as they do today, but from the various elected magistrates, particularly provincial governors, the aediles, and (most important) the praetors. These orders are called "edicts," from their Latin name, which means something spoken out loud. Originally, these presumably were spoken orders directed at some immediate audience (say, ordering a crowd to disperse or a man to hand over a disputed piece of property). By recorded times, however, edicts had generally come to be written orders binding on the general public. In principle, they were valid only for the magistrate's year in office. Romans spoke of these edicts as "supplementing" the statute law (say, by filling in gaps or simply by adding mechanisms of enforcement), but we will see in the final section of this chapter that the relationship between the two was more complicated than that. Once emperors started issuing decrees of lasting validity, the traditional type of edict became much less important (but see the following section on the edict of the urban praetor).

Statute law was written to be general law, just as most laws are today, and many edicts had equally broad applications. But it is impossible for the writers of legislation (now or then) to foresee exactly how their law might apply to every real-world

ROMAN LAW AND THE LEGAL WORLD OF THE ROMANS

situation that might eventually arise. It is not even clear that lawmakers always do their best in this regard. Hence, someone must decide how the general law is to apply in specific cases. In the United States, this is primarily the job of the courts. While the Roman courts necessarily had some such role, the main work of interpretation was left to a group called "jurists." The nature of this profession will be discussed at length in Chapter 5, but for now we can just think of them as somewhat similar to modern law professors. Roman courts had to apply the law in specific cases, but they did not publish decisions, as American courts can, so it was hard for a decision in one case to affect that in another. Jurists published their own interpretations of the laws (and of each other) both in general terms and in specific cases. Over time, these decisions came to shape the law a great deal (the full extent will be discussed in the last section. By contrast, Roman courts did not explain their rulings either orally or in writing.) During the Imperial period, the emperors' "responses" could offer authoritative interpretations of (and even amendments to) the law, but juristic activity continued to be important until the early third century AD. Even after juristic production slowed, the jurists' body of written work continued to be influential (see Chapter 3 on the *Digest*).

"THE EDICT"

One particular source of law among those just described was so important that it deserves its own section. Among the various officials who could publish edicts was the city praetor of Rome, generally called the "urban praetor" after his Latin title. Much of Roman private law came from his edict (which was itself a collection of many edicts on various topics). Some major areas of law, such as contract and defamation, were governed almost entirely by this edict. When legal scholars speak simply of "the Edict," they are referring to the edict of the urban praetor. We noted earlier that an edict was technically valid only so long as the magistrate issuing it was in office. This could have made for a very unstable legal situation, but in practice each urban praetor tended to re-enact all (or nearly all) of his predecessor's edict. When necessary, changes could be made without cumbersome legislative action, but generally the tradition was quite conservative. (The same traditional practice applied to the edicts of the other magistrates, at least in Rome, e.g., [4].)[1]

It did not take long for the emperors to remove even this small amount of discretion from the urban praetors. By about AD 130, the form of the Edict was declared fixed (though the emperors themselves retained the power to order changes). At the same time, there was no particular attempt to replace the Edict with imperial laws in other forms. Hence, the urban praetor's edict remained central to Roman law for centuries after individual praetors had ceased to have any power over the legal system.

The content of the Edict mostly took the form of a list of "actions" the praetor would grant to plaintiffs. That is, it was

---

[1] Numbers in boldface and square brackets refer to the collection of translated documents at the end of the book.

not framed in terms of general legal rights or principles. Rather, it specified the remedies that would be available in many particular situations. A more detailed discussion of these actions will be found in Chapter 11, but a few words may be in order here. In some cases, the Edict just specified the circumstances in which the praetor would grant a trial (in modern terms, various "causes of action"). In other cases, he specified the "formulae" that could actually be used in those circumstances – directions to judges on how to decide various kinds of cases. There were also standard orders the praetor might issue himself. These included simple commands, for example, requiring a builder to give insurance against damage to neighboring property, prerequisites to being allowed to initiate a suit, or a conditional command called an "interdict" (e.g., to restore possession of an item [if] taken by force; see also Chapter 13 on the law of property). He could also decree a *restitutio in integrum*, a decree that nullified some pre-existing transaction.

RELATIONSHIP BETWEEN SOURCES

In the American system, decrees (say, the rules of federal agencies) and precedent/interpretation are generally meant to be subordinate to statute law. Romans sometimes speak as if they imagined a similar hierarchy; one lawyer said that the edicts were meant to "assist, supplement, and correct" the core of the statute law, what they sometimes called the *ius civile*, lumping together all statute law, regardless of source. But actual practice looks much more complicated than that. Let us consider first the relationship between statute law and edicts, then the even more complicated issue of the "interpretation" of both.

In some instances, it seems that edictal law exists only to implement statute law. So, for instance, the edict specifies the action to use in suing a thief. Theft was already recognized as an offense in statute law, but your property rights meant nothing in the Roman system if there was no specific action to defend them. (In fact, the Romans tended not even to talk about "rights" in the modern sense, just actions.) In other cases, the edict expanded the scope of already-existing statute law. For instance, legislation of the mid fifth century BC allowed suits to recover for bodily injury; the Edict eventually extended this protection to mere insult. In still others, the rules of the edict practically changed the statute law. (Technically, the old rules were not abolished. The praetor simply announced that he would make a new system available). The praetor effectively changed the rules of inheritance by simply granting the right to sue for part of the estate to new classes of relatives (see Chapter 15). He could perhaps have been overruled in this by the passage of a new statute, but we have no examples of that happening. And finally, there were areas in which the praetor simply created the law out of whole cloth. The most notable of these was the creation of the binding consensual contract (Chapter 12).

Both statute law and edicts were subject to interpretation by the jurists, and interpretation could have much the same range of effects on both that edicts could have on statute law.

Interpretation was often framed as "definition" of specific words in the underlying law, but jurists sometimes allowed themselves enormous freedom within that rhetorical framework. Before discussing the more adventurous cases, let me mention two circumstances in which interpretation would be required by any lights. First, Roman laws (of whatever sort) did not generally come with built-in definitions; contrast modern statutes, which are full of them. So a law protected the owner of "herd animals" (*pecudes*) from "wrongful killing" of those animals. In Rome's early days, the term "herd animals" was largely clear (though there was controversy over pigs), but the jurists had to be called in eventually to settle whether elephants were covered. Second, in any system interpreters may need to be called in to clean up after legal documents were poorly written. For instance, lawyers wondered what do to with a promise "that a product was of good quality." If it turned out to be defective, the promise would be for an "impossibility," like a car that will take you to the moon, and so invalid. (It would be better, they thought, to use a promise to pay a penalty if it wasn't; [4] seems to do both).

In cases such as these, as I noted, the need for interpretation is fairly clear. But often it was used to make bigger changes than were necessary to solve particular problems, and sometimes the purported definition or interpretation seems completely unmotivated. So, for instance, the Edict gives an action to enforce contractual sale without spelling out most of the rules that govern buying and selling. Instead of being added in some form, they were brought in as part of the "definition" of sale. The rule, for instance, that sale must involve a cash price (i.e., trades do not count) might make sense as a definition, but the idea that certain warranties are also part of the meaning of the term "sale" seems very forced. Even stranger, perhaps, are cases such as the rule on how to free children from their parents' control. There was a clear statutory rule that sons could be freed by being sold off three times (how they would come back after the first two times is not relevant here). The interpreters could have decided that "son" stood for "son or daughter" and left well enough alone, or they could have said that daughters were not included at all, since they weren't literally mentioned. Either would clearly be "interpretation" in the usual modern sense. Instead, they asserted that "three times" was a special case for male children and that the unwritten "normal" rule for everyone else (i.e., only daughters) involved being sold only once. This kind of "interpretation" is used to generate an entirely novel rule.

4. SOURCES FOR ROMAN LAW

❖❖❖❖❖❖❖❖

To FIND OUT today's law on a given topic, there are many resources available. The governmental agencies that make the laws have standard places in which to publish them. Commercial publishers collect and distribute the same material (with or without additional information), both on paper and now on-line. Libraries, some general-purpose and others specializing in law, collect these materials. Enthusiastic amateurs and, increasingly, search engines make the texts even more broadly available. To discover Roman law is often a more difficult matter. The bulk of this chapter will discuss the main sources available to us, but it will be worthwhile to begin by noting the kinds of problems we face.

The first and most important problem is one that affects historians asking virtually any question about the Roman world. Most of the evidence available, even to the Romans themselves, was in the form of documents written on paperlike materials. But these typically do not survive the centuries needed to come into our hands. In a few lucky cases, texts were popular enough to be copied and recopied through the ages, but this is rare and still leaves other problems (to be discussed later). A second problem has to do with the sources initially available. Ancient governments did not necessarily make arrangements for wide publication of their laws in the way that modern ones do, nor were there private institutions to publish, circulate, or even centralize legal documents. For instance, a famous letter exchange between a provincial governor and the emperor in the early second century AD indicates that neither had an archive of previous imperial decisions affecting the province. Many documents were published in a few copies on lasting media, and there were a few central archives. However, neither the original completeness of those collections, nor their preservation, nor their retrieval systems were remotely up to modern standards.

Essentially the same problem exists for the writings of the jurists. Moreover, there is a special problem related to legal texts not encountered in most other kinds of historical evidence. Romans, of course, were generally interested in legal writings not because they were part of "history," but because they were "law." Their interests were practical, not academic. Not only did they usually omit information that was "merely" historical, but legal texts were sometimes actually rewritten (usually without warning) to accommodate changes in the law. (This rewriting is called "interpolation.") Contrast, say, the way we keep track of the American Constitution. Looking at the text, we can see that slavery was originally recognized in the United States but was eventually abolished (by the Thirteenth Amendment). This kind of historical perspective is often lost in Roman texts.

TECHNICAL SOURCES (REFERENCE)

Despite these problems, scholars have been able to reconstruct a remarkable amount of information about Roman law. In this section and the next, I will discuss technical sources, that is, documents produced by or for legal experts or at least as part of the legal process. These technical sources will be further divided into reference texts (those designed to record and explain the law in general) and documentary ones (i.e., documents actually used as part of particular transactions). Then, in the last section, I will discuss nontechnical sources – what information can we get from texts that were not originally meant to be "legal" such as histories, plays, and letters?

The texts of the majority of Roman statute laws are lost to us, and for the remainder we generally have only partial quotations or paraphrase. The best-preserved single law from the Republic comes to us inscribed on a broken bronze plaque. We can tell from the shape of the remains that less than half the text survives. A few imperial enactments are better preserved and/or found in more than one copy, but the general situation is not really any better. Moreover, the best-preserved texts often have a limited, local application. A provincial city would have good reason to publish an imperial decree freeing it from taxation, but no community would have a similar reason to spend a lot of time and money to inscribe the legal rules regarding theft. Far more common than the preservation of large fragments on stone or bronze is the quotation of a few words or sentences in the juristic works to be discussed later.

The situation of the text of the Edict is roughly similar. On the one hand, there are not even limited inscribed records (just as we would expect for such general texts). On the other, the Edict is more systematically quoted by the jurists. One form in which they wrote was the commentary on major bodies of law. The centrality and compactness of the Edict made it an attractive framework for this, especially once it had been fixed by the emperor. Thus we can reverse-engineer much of the Edict with some confidence.

Another important type of legal writing was the introductory textbook. Two of these survive more or less complete, both with the general title *Institutiones* ("Training," a title used for education in other fields as well). The earlier of these appears to come from the mid second century AD and was written by a jurist known only by his first name, Gaius (rather like referring to a modern legal expert simply as "John"). We know essentially nothing about him personally. The work offers a systematic but reasonably accessible treatment of most of Roman private law; the areas he does not treat at all – notably what we might today call criminal, constitutional, and religious law – appear to have been similarly (if less dramatically) neglected by the rest of the profession. Gaius is more distinctive in giving, if only occasionally, information about the law before his own time that could only have been of historical interest. We are lucky to have the work at all; it comes from a single manuscript that has some gaps and whose pages were reused to write other works on. The other textbook comes down to us under the name of the sixth-century emperor Justinian (see the later discussion of its real authorship), and in many respects is simply an updated revision of Gaius's work.

Mention of Justinian leads us to the most important technical source (or set of sources): the so-called *Corpus Iuris Civilis* (literally the "body of the civil law"). This was a set of four legal works prepared in the 530s AD at the direction of the Byzantine (i.e., Eastern Roman) emperor Justinian. The revised *Institutiones* were one of its components, and two of the others are relatively unimportant for our purposes. The fourth component, however, is far and away our most important single source for Roman law. It is called the *Digest*, and it is (as the name suggests) a compilation work. Justinian's chief lawyer, Tribonian, and a committee sorted through the texts of centuries of juristic writings, gathering together the relevant passages on various topics, and selecting and (sometimes) editing them to give up-to-date information. The idea was that this officially approved collection would then replace the original juristic texts and even the statutory law and edictal material they quoted and discussed. This project is helpful to the modern historian in that it was designed to be broad and systematic. It has also proven handy that Tribonian and his team worked as quickly as they did; apparently it took them only about three years to process thousands of "books" of raw material. This was reduced to fifty books (each the length of a long modern chapter and divided into subsections called "titles"). They did not have time to smooth out differences between individual jurists or even between whole periods of law nearly as much as their mission would have suggested. Instead of a smooth, unified legal code, we have a document that shows its origins in cut-and-paste. Moreover, the editors were very good about providing citations for the passages they quote, aiding in our reconstructions of who said what and when. The disadvantage of the project from a modern point of view is that the *Digest* rendered all the early material – statutory, edictal, and juristic alike – purely historical. As a result, none of it survives in its original form. The other parts of the *Corpus* were slightly less efficient in eliminating their predecessors but still left little behind. The *Corpus* remained of sufficient importance for long enough that it was preserved by copying (first in religious settings, later in the earliest European universities), just as the major literary works of antiquity were.

In addition to the major works just discussed, we also get occasional nuggets of information from lesser and later technical works. Some later collections of imperial enactments have also survived, as well as late and summary juristic works.

TECHNICAL SOURCES (DOCUMENTARY)

The documentary sources are the scraps of contracts, receipts, wills, arbiters' decisions, property markers, and other documents that were once part of actual business transactions or legal proceedings and that have now survived as historical evidence. Such documents can survive for two different reasons. In some cases, it is because they were written on particularly lasting materials such as stone or metal tablets. For instance, we know the contents of the will of a man usually called Dasumius (d. AD 108) because he made provisions for it to be inscribed on stone and made public. (This was apparently part of a more general goal of memorialization after death.) However, the process was expensive and time-consuming, so inscriptions were usually reserved for things like laws and treaties instead of day-to-day legal documents. The other reason for preservation is that peculiar local conditions sometimes happened to promote the survival of more common, but normally more perishable, writing surfaces: papyrus, parchment (both essentially forms of paper), and wax tablets. The most important example of this is the way the dryness of the Egyptian desert has preserved thousands of documents (legal and nonlegal) written on papyrus.

Because the survival of documentary sources depends so much on random circumstance, the information we get from them is potentially distorted. For instance, documents from anywhere in Egypt may be unrepresentative because we know that that area had an unusual legal system, combining elements of Roman, Greek, and native Egyptian law (see Chapter 21). Or consider the records recovered from the area around Pompeii and Herculaneum in central Italy that was buried by the eruption of Vesuvius in AD 79. On the one hand, both legal scholars and archaeologists benefit from having a "snapshot" of these cities at a particular moment in time. On the other, the surviving records may be idiosyncratic. We have several hundred documents, but they are nearly all from only two archives (in and near Pompeii) and a third cluster of records (at Herculaneum).

That is, we have the business records (which are presumably not complete) of only a few people among the tens of thousands who lived in the area at the time of the eruption, to say nothing of the tens of millions who lived under Roman law at one time or another. There are a few similar caches from other times and places (most notably one found in modern-day Transylvania), but the essential problem remains. Because we have so little hard evidence, it is hard to tell whether any given piece of it is "normal" or, if so, how far we can generalize it in time or space. Still, the documentary evidence has the advantage of being real. We need not worry about problems like interpolation or the danger that our reference sources, even if we know what they mean to say, are too theoretical. Arguably, the law that governs day-to-day life is the most important law, even if it is not officially "correct." Hence many of the example texts will be drawn from documentary sources, and especially from the principal Pompeian archive.

NONTECHNICAL SOURCES

The "nontechnical" sources are a very mixed bag, including virtually everything else that gives us some information about the law. Given what survives from ancient Rome, that generally means literary texts. Almost anything can make reference to the law, but a few categories are of special importance.

The first of these is antiquarian writing. By the time we start to have a good quantity of surviving texts (the first century

BC), the Roman state was already more than half a millennium old. The Romans, a people who put a lot of stock in "tradition," were interested in their own history, even if they were not always well informed. Hence we have works like Marcus Terentius Varro's *Human and Divine Antiquities* (mid first century BC), which was (as the title suggests) entirely an investigation into Roman traditions, and Aulus Gellius's *Attic Nights* (mid second century AD), in which he copies and comments on interesting things he has read, including legal matters. There are many problems associated with these antiquarian works. It is not always clear when an ancient story reflects a legal point at all, and it is often hard to tell whether our sources (and their sources, and theirs, and so on) have correctly understood whatever legal content there was. After all, these authors were leisured gentlemen, not professional lawyers or historians. And, sadly, most of Varro's work is in any case now lost.

In a similar vein, we might look to "history" proper, that is, to works that tell of the past in continuous narratives rather than as collections of miscellaneous facts. The situation here is often even worse than with the antiquarians. In antiquity, history was a highly literary genre, greatly shaped by considerations of style and "appropriateness," written by amateurs. They did not necessarily know or even care about the law. So, to take a very simple example, our sources for celebrated criminal trials do not always even agree on what the defendant was charged with.

It may seem surprising to us, but a better source for many things may come from Roman comedy (plays that were not unlike their eventual descendent, the TV sit-com). It was not uncommon for characters in these plays to comment on legalities or at least to use legal language. Also, the surviving comedies happen to come from a period (late third and early second century BC) for which we have very little other evidence. For the historian, this kind of text presents an obvious problem. A joke doesn't need to get the law exactly right to be funny. It is not, for instance, really illegal for the owner to remove the tag from his or her mattress, as many comedians suggest. Still, at the very least, comedy can be used to date legal institutions that we understand better from other sources. For instance, a law against "going around with a weapon" that would otherwise be dated to the first century BC can be placed at least a century earlier because a character quotes a phrase from it.

My last and probably most important category is of a somewhat different sort. It includes the various writings of the politician, orator, and legal hobbyist Marcus Tullius Cicero (106–43 BC). Cicero was a practicing courtroom advocate, and after courtroom successes he often published the speeches he had given at trial. Though probably edited somewhat for publication and preserved for us by generations of copying, these come close to being documentary sources. They share the advantages and disadvantages of that kind of evidence. On the one hand, they are biased (he's trying to win) and incomplete (he's arguing one case, not teaching a class), and in general it is hard to tell how representative any particular item is. On the other, they have some of the same claims to "reality" that more humble documents have. Beyond the speeches, however, many of Cicero's other writings are of occasional legal interest. His surviving letters to friends and family often touch on legal matters, sometimes in considerable detail. His philosophical and rhetorical treaties also include legal discussions, both as main topics (e.g., the obligations of contracts) and as incidental illustrations of other points (e.g., how to organize a speech that relies on definition).

5. THE LEGAL PROFESSIONS

✧✧✧✧✧✧✧✧

A ROMAN FACING a legal problem might be assisted by two different kinds of professionals (or, if not literally professionals, at least experts): an advocate, whose training and experience were primarily in public speaking, and a "jurist," whose role was primarily in interpreting and explaining the law. The first section will sketch out the differences between the two (which changed somewhat over time). The second will discuss ways in which the two remained somewhat connected to each other. The last briefly treats a few other types of legal workers.

THE TWO PROFESSIONS

Aquilius Gallus, a legal expert of the mid first century BC, made himself available to answer legal questions from strangers. When asked about handling questions of fact that arose in particular cases, he is said to have answered: "That is not a question for the law; it is a question for Cicero." While he framed the matter as a difference between persons (himself and

Cicero), it is generally believed that he was pointing to a more general distinction between (to use the English terms) "jurists" and "advocates."

In Latin, jurists could be referred to by a number of different phrases meaning roughly "expert in law." According to a comment of Cicero's elsewhere, these experts made themselves useful through pleading, consulting (as Aquilius did with his visitors), and legal drafting. Pleading in court seems to have fallen away over time (though this can be disputed), but advice and even providing evidence in individual cases continued. Additionally (and most visibly to us), jurists came to publish their legal opinions. This could take the form of writing down the results of their original oral consultations, offering commentary on major legal texts (say, the Twelve Tables or the Edict), or composing treatises on specific topics (say, the criminal law or the duties of provincial governors). In any of its forms, their work tended to be patronal rather than professional. That is, they provided such help out of a sense of public duty, to aid friends, and/or to gain prestige, rather than to make a living. Someone who acted as an "advocate" in court might use that very term to describe his role in a particular trial, but might usually prefer the broader "orator" if asked to describe himself elsewhere. And, in fact, it was quite likely that he did use his skills as a speaker in other, typically political spheres. He usually came from an elevated social group in which rhetorical education was the standard form of higher education. If he needed specialist legal knowledge in a particular case, he could consult a jurist. Like the jurists, advocates generally did not work for a fee. In fact, during many periods it was illegal to pay one's advocate, though the restriction was easily and commonly evaded.

SOME COMPLICATIONS

What I have just described is the traditional picture. While it seems to be true in general terms, the situation was probably also a little messier. To illustrate this, it will be necessary to trace the history of both "professions" over time. However, before discussing these, I need to say a few words about the general nature of professionalism in the Roman world. First, it is important to note that Rome was not very bureaucratized in this respect (as in others). That is, there were no government agencies or semiprivate institutions (like, say, bar associations in law or accrediting associations in higher education) to certify who was a legitimate member of any profession, at least until the very late years of the empire (see the next chapter), and even then it was rare. Second, work in the area of the law was generally reserved for members of the political, social, and economic elite. It was customary within this group to spread the idea that personal character was more important than expertise in any specific area. So, for instance, jobs within the government were largely assigned by seniority and by lot rather than by any demonstrable competence. Famously, Servius Sulpicius Rufus, the most distinguished legal expert of his day, was praetor in 65 BC but was not put in charge of the civil courts (as urban praetor) because his lot did not come up. Thus it was not in the interest of elites to promote an emphasis on credentialing in any profession. Moreover, members of this elite class did not depend on any profession to make a living; they had inherited wealth. Picking one job or another would tie them down unnecessarily. Thus, on the one hand, advocates were not required to be legal experts (and vice versa), but, on the other, there were no institutions to prevent a given person from entering both arenas.

The normal Latin word for an advocate (at least on the defendant's side) was "patron," a term that carried much broader social implications. A patron (the word comes from the word for "father") was a social superior who was supposed to look out for a set of social inferiors ("clients"), who were in turn loyal to and supportive of him. In principle, this relationship should be long-standing and inclusive of many activities: advice (both legal and practical), gift giving, access to persons of different social ranks. In this context, the patron would be more likely to have access to legal knowledge than his clients, both by virtue of better general education and by being part of or connected to the governmental apparatus. Still, the most important thing a patron brought to a case might well be his personal authority rather than his specific legal knowledge. If authority and knowledge became somewhat confused with each other, that worked to the patron's advantage. It personalized something (legal expertise) that could otherwise be seen as an unfairly distributed resource. Also, the practice differed somewhat from the principle, at least by the later Republic. While defense speakers liked the prestige generated by posing as generous or civic-minded "patrons," they were in fact engaged on a case-by-case basis and normally expected some concrete show of the client's gratitude.

Prosecution was traditionally the domain of men of lesser standing because of their youth and/or lower birth, though exceptions on both scores were more numerous than has sometimes been suggested. The difference seems to be that defense produced friends, prosecution made enemies. Prosecution was largely left to those who needed to make a splash. Over time, patronage became less coherent, but no less important. Public speaking in general, whether in the courts, political venues, or ceremonial contexts, remained a multipurpose skill for social and political advancement.

It is an open question how much law an advocate needed to know to be effective in his job, and in fact the issue was controversial in antiquity. A number of sources from the mid first century BC to the early second AD discuss the issue, all from the point of view of advocates, rather than that of lawyers. Despite this uniformity, there was a considerable diversity of opinion on the question of legal knowledge. Some felt the good advocate would have a systematic (if not fully expert) knowledge of the law. Others thought legal knowledge was largely irrelevant, could be sought by consultation on individual cases, or could even be counterproductive. Unfortunately, all these writers seem to be more concerned with reputation than practicality. Does it make oratory *look* better if it absorbs and subordinates the law, or if it can dismiss it altogether? The one thing this debate does show us clearly is that the distinction between advocates and jurists was not entirely imaginary, even given the lack of institutional distinctions. They really were rivals, so they must have been fairly distinct, even if some individuals crossed the line.

The nature of the juristic "profession" seems to have changed more over time that that of the advocates. In the earliest days, certain priests (the so-called pontiffs) were both the keepers and interpreters of the laws. Sacred and secular law, however, seem to have split apart centuries before our period, leaving most interpretation in the hands of a much less well-defined group of elites. (The supposed religious origins of the legal system may have had some lasting effect on *styles* of interpretation, but the formal role of the pontiffs had been entirely eliminated by historical times.) During the subsequent years of the Republic, legal interpretation and advice seem to have been largely considered patronal duties (and prerogatives), much like advocacy. Advocates and legal experts at least came from the same class, and particular individuals might well appeal to the same patron for both functions. Starting perhaps in the mid second century BC, there was a gradual creation of a more distinct juristic role. This involved multiple overlapping changes. Within the law, published and circulated opinions (and other writings) became more important, and at the same time there was an emphasis on a somewhat more systematic approach to the law. Outside the law, the men who wrote and read these works were increasingly willing to stake their social position on their legal abilities rather than on their broader patronal duties. Along with these trends, some have detected another. It may be the case that these jurists were of a slightly lower social status than the aristocrats who had dispensed legal advice in previous generations; such men would still have ready access to legal resources, but would be risking less by employing such a specialist strategy. Thus the class of "jurists" became somewhat more clearly defined than that of "advocates," though still not precisely fixed, nor formally opposed to the latter group.

These trends continued into the first century AD, but the Empire also brought a new development of its own. As the justice system came under the control of the emperors, it was professionalized (and "professional" now becomes a more literally accurate term). Leading jurists were hired into government positions. While the Republican posts with influence over the law, most notably the urban praetorship, were not normally filled by experts, the corresponding imperial jobs (say, the urban and praetorian prefects) were. And while these jurists carried out their official responsibilities, they did not cease to publish, at least not immediately. Eventually, in the early to mid third century AD, this public activity fell off dramatically. Jurists could practice, teach, and hold office, but they had largely ceased to be an independently creative part of the legal system. This, along with a more systematic training in both professions (see the next chapter), brought them back together, at least to some extent. While there does not yet seem to have been licensing to enter either profession, we know that those who had proven themselves morally unfit might eventually be banned from practicing law. In this context, it is worth noting that jurists and advocates were similar enough that the same offenses would get you banned from both jobs, but different enough that a rule had to be made to state the point explicitly.

OTHER TERMINOLOGY

Most of the discussion to this point has described the situation at the top (socially speaking) of both professions. There is some evidence, however, that there were other types of legal practitioners, some defined primarily in functional terms, others in social. On the one hand, surviving records of particular cases (almost entirely from Egypt) show us the intervention of advocates at much lower social levels than we have been talking about. On the other hand, we also have occasional references to terminology for different professionals who might carry out that kind of work. For instance, there are the so-called *pragmatici* or "men of affairs." The word is Greek in origin, and the majority of instances refer to Greek contexts, but they seem to have existed in the Roman world as well. *Pragmatici* appear to have been legal experts in the employ of speakers. They differ from jurists in (perhaps) not publishing, in working for a wage, and (we may suspect from the last) in being of lower social standing. The so-called *causidici* perhaps stood in the same relationship to elite advocates as *pragmatici* did to elite jurists. The term means simply "pleaders of cases." *Causidici* are associated with members of other socially suspect professions, such as heralds and auctioneers, and with nonprofessional loudmouths. Like the *pragmatici*, they are spoken of as working for wages, which again suggests a class distinction. At least one elite author admits there is no significant functional distinction. It has been suggested that there was more mobility between functions at this level than at the top of the professions. While this is entirely plausible, there really isn't enough evidence to tell.

Somewhat different from these two groups are the *formularii* or *legulei*. The terms are derived from the *formula* at the heart of civil procedure (see Chapter 11) and the basic word for "law." On the one hand, *formularii* are, like the *causidici*, associated with some less-than-respectable professions. On the other, there does seem to be a functional difference. They seem to be specialists even within the law, worrying over the details of legal drafting. Perhaps the same is true for the even less well-attested *tabelliones* ("tablet men").

Because of the nature of the evidence, it has been necessary to speak of these lower-status professionals as being at the margins of the system. In some respects that may be accurate; they did not shape the monuments of the law (statutes, edicts, juristic commentary) like the better-known advocates and jurists. At the same time, most people who had contact with the legal system presumably did not do so through the ancient equivalents of celebrity lawyers and Harvard law professors. They went to the local man who had spent time in courts or had helped a neighbor draft a will or contract. Thus these "minor" figures may actually have been the real face of Roman law.

6. LEGAL EDUCATION

❧❧❧❧❧❧❧❧❧

I BEGIN THIS CHAPTER with three very general observations. (1) While Roman education took on mostly Greek forms, education in the law had no real Greek precedents. Formal legal education is thus generally thought of as Rome's great innovation in pedagogy. (2) While basic literacy was expected of women of the upper classes in Rome, and while a few even became quite learned on their own, they were cut off from most advanced education by custom. Moreover, they were banned from most courtroom activity by rule. Hence, the references below to "men," "sons," "he," and so forth are meant to have their full, gendered force. (3) The evidence for Roman legal education is a little peculiar. We have essentially two snapshots of standard practices at two particular times – the late Republic and the later Empire – and a slightly broader but also less detailed view of what went on in the first two centuries of the Empire. We have virtually no information on the transitions between these phases. In what follows, I will simply treat the three phases in chronological order.

Before discussing Republican legal education, it is important first to know a few things about Republican education more generally. By the later part of the Republic (if not much before), the formal education of the Roman upper classes had become fairly standardized. We are speaking here not only of the minute group of perhaps a few thousand families whose sons might possibly have had a political career in Rome, but also about the merely well-to-do. This group is much larger – several percent of the population – and defined almost entirely by wealth rather than by status or connections. There were no state schools; instruction was provided either by freelance instructors who scheduled classes whenever and wherever they were able or, for the wealthiest, by private tutors owned or hired for the purpose. Though a few elementary mathematical skills and the like were taught in the early years, secondary and post-secondary instruction was almost entirely devoted to literacy and to literary skills, such as reading, analyzing, and sometimes composing various kinds of literary texts. Those who went on with their schooling followed up with instruction in the art of public speaking. This standard curriculum ran until the late teens. Afterward, there were several different training options for the well-to-do young man. Military service (with rank dependent on status) was a prerequisite for a political career. Advanced instruction in rhetoric, as well as in more specialized subjects such as philosophy, was available in Greece and, increasingly, from Greeks who had come to Rome. Most importantly, the sons of the well connected would be informally apprenticed to the most prominent figures who were agreeable. This practice, not unlike a modern internship, was sometimes referred to as the *tirocinium fori* (roughly, "political boot camp"). During this period, the younger man would follow the elder as the latter carried out his daily business, both public and private. There was no formal instruction, but presumably explanations would be offered as necessary and as time allowed. This gave the "apprentice" close contact with business, political, and legal affairs. Different people went through various combinations of these academic, military, and political options in their late teens and early twenties.

It is in the context of this *tirocinium* that law was generally taught during the late Republic. That is, you learned the law by being attached to someone who himself practiced a lot of legal business. We are told by Marcus Tullius Cicero (106–43 BC), eventually a statesman, trial advocate, and skilled amateur in the law, that he had had to memorize Rome's first law code, the Twelve Tables, in his school days. There is no indication, however, that this was treated as anything but a patriotic relic, and at any rate he suggests that the practice had been discontinued. When Cicero spoke of learning real-world legal skills, he described his teenage experiences following two men named Quintus Mucius Scaevola (who were perhaps cousins to each other), the preeminent jurists of their time. It is perhaps worth noting that neither Cicero nor any of his immediate "classmates" went on to juristic careers; even with the Scaevolas, legal training was merely part of a broader preparation for a career in what we would call politics. Becoming a jurist oneself was a matter of individual study and writing and face-to-face interaction with those already in place. In addition to offering purely practical experience, the mentor was presumably also able to make specialized legal texts available to his protégés. This was a world without much in the way of a book trade, especially for nonliterary works. Finding an obscure legal text was a matter of knowing the author (or knowing someone who knew the author, or someone else in the chain). Unlike the core curriculum of literature and public speaking, legal training of this sort required connections, not just money. Cicero's connection to the Scaevolas was via his main mentor, Lucius Licinius Crassus (consul in 95 BC), who was a connection of his father's (though we don't know exactly how). Cicero's family was very important in his small hometown, but it seems unlikely that most similarly situated young men would have had the same kind of access.

In the early years of the Empire, and in one case even as far back as the reign of the very first emperor, more formalized schools of law appear for the first time. Two were especially prominent: the "followers of Sabinus" and the "followers of Proculus." We know of them both from narrative accounts and from records of particular disagreements on points of legal doctrine. It has been claimed that these were mainly "schools of thought," but it is likely that they were educational institutions as well. Though the names usually given ("followers of") are ambiguous, we occasionally see references that are more explicit. The existence of a series of "heads" for both also suggests an institutional context. Their legal disputes also seem not to have been based on any deep principles, which might also suggest that they were schools in the institutional sense, not the philosophical. Pliny the Younger, a letter writer of the early second century AD, also tells us explicitly of a nearly contemporary legal school, attached to a man named Cassius, that is probably identical with the "Sabinian" school, and at the very least represents a distinct school of the educational sort. Two other writers of roughly the same period allude to teaching centers in Rome, which may well also be educational institutions. Finally, from the middle of the second century, we have a surviving introductory legal textbook – *Institutes* – in four "books." (An ancient "book" is roughly equivalent to a long chapter today.) This was written by a jurist known only by his first name, Gaius. It is a broad but terse summary of much of Roman civil law. We also know of an apparently very similar work from the first half of the first century by Masurius Sabinus, the namesake of the Sabinian school. Either book would have to have been accompanied by considerable oral instruction of some type, again pointing to an organized school. While the evidence gives us some confidence in the existence of law schools, only Gaius tells us much about how they operated. Presumably there were lectures. There could have been discussion of a more Socratic sort. There is no evidence for discussion of historical cases as in modern law schools. There could have been "mock trial" exercises, though the evidence for those is as a part of the schools of rhetoric, not of law. In short, we don't know what the students were required to do or to produce.

Whatever the details of procedure in the schools, several big-picture issues can be raised about them. The first has to do with the many famous jurists associated with the two named schools. Teaching in Rome had traditionally been a job for persons of lower status (including slaves and former slaves). Is it really likely that prominent men, many of them holders of public offices, including the consulship, would have been regular lecturers? There was some change in the general pattern in the first century. The emperor Vespasian created public professors of rhetoric in the 70s. Moreover, this establishment can be seen in the context of the creation of a whole range of salaried imperial offices during this period. The status of these positions is ambiguous. On the one hand, the connection to the center of power elevates them. On the other, the formal dependency on the emperor limits it. Thus these positions were normally held not by the highest social class (the senators), but by the next group down (equestrians; see Chapter 6 for more on the distinction). Now, we also know that jurists of the earlier Empire were more likely to come from this second class than jurists of the late Republic. Yet among the purported heads of the two schools, a few were from distinguished families, and most came to hold the consulship. Thus, whatever their origins, they would likely have felt that they'd moved up in the world. In this context, one of these teaching positions would amount to a demotion for many of these elite jurists, or at least an unwanted reminder of earlier days. And at any rate, state professorships of law did not come into being until well after those for rhetoric.

It has been plausibly suggested that formal instruction in the early Imperial law schools would have been in the hands of a lower tier of jurists whose names are now lost. Moreover, the need for numbers would in any case require us to assume that some unknown instructors existed. The noble men who served as heads of the schools would then have held largely honorific positions, and would have interacted with students (when they did so at all) in a manner that mimicked the Republican *tirocinium fori*. Still, the existence of formal schools would presumably have expanded the availability of legal education. Admittance to study would presumably have required money, both indirectly (in the form of good primary and secondary instruction) and directly (since the teachers were not generally state-sponsored). Still, the schools could *create* the set of connections with the legal establishment that the earlier Republican system wanted as a prerequisite instead.

This situation seems to hold until at least the mid second century, and probably until much later than that. Our next clear look at legal instruction comes from imperial decrees of the fifth and sixth centuries. This is after the period covered in most of this book, but it may show us conditions that had come into being somewhat earlier. At any rate, we now find several distinctive features. There are major schools in Rome, Beirut (this one going back at least to 239), and Constantinople (modern Istanbul in Turkey, and then the capital of the eastern half of the empire), as well as less important ones elsewhere around the empire. The major schools were headed by state-sponsored professors, though the bulk of instruction was still in the hands of "private" lecturers attached to the schools. Most notably, a fixed curriculum was established by law (though its content may have been traditional for some time before then). For each of five years, there were specified readings: synthetic instructional works in the first year and more professional works later. Most of these texts were centuries-old "classics," though legal writings were often subject to ongoing modification ("interpolation") to keep them current. There is even evidence that standard editions of the texts were produced for use in the schools, a practice otherwise nearly unheard of in the ancient book trade. For the first three years there were public lectures, though all five years presumably included slightly less formal instruction.

While we do not know much about the chronology of the bureaucratization of the law schools or their spread into the provinces, we can say a little about the forces likely to have brought them about. First, while never static, the state of the law had stabilized. The most important source of law, the Praetor's Edict, had finally been fixed in the first half of the second century. Once citizenship was granted to all free persons in the empire in AD 212, the whole Roman world was, at least in theory, subject to a single legal regime. Roman law had always been primarily about Roman citizens (see Chapter 21); now that meant everybody. The age of productive jurisprudence came to an end in the first half of the third century (note that this is the end date of most of the textbooks mentioned above). If the law was less of a "moving target," it was easier to make instruction more systematic. Late imperial culture as a whole is also described as increasingly bureaucratic, both in the growth of the state apparatus and in attempts by the state to impose its order on the rest of society. This is particularly relevant to the law schools because they came to serve a credentialing function in the later empire (at least in the eastern part). A law degree was required to practice before the higher courts, and this was in turn a qualification for positions in government.

Still, this elaborate system may represent only a very partial picture. Though much larger than the Republican and early Imperial governments, the Late Antique state apparatus was still tiny compared to modern governments. It could have absorbed only so many men with legal training. They must have been vastly outnumbered by lesser legal professionals who worked as private counsel throughout the empire. Conversely, it seems unlikely that the great schools could have produced all of these. I have already mentioned the existence, only barely attested, of lower-tier law schools in the provinces, and there must have been many more of these that have left no trace, even in Italy. It is also possible that many may have learned as apprentices, not on the model of the old elite acculturation of future aristocrats, but more like tradesmen. The same could well be true of our two earlier periods as well. There was apparently significant civil litigation among the merely well-to-do of Cicero's age. They must have had access to some kind of legal advisors. We have little direct evidence of individual cases, but this was presumably the function of the "lesser" juristic types such as *tabelliones*, *formularii*, and *causidici* (see Chapter 5). We have better individual attestation of rhetorically trained advocates at this social level.) Similarly, the great schools of the early Empire could not have served the needs of a rapidly growing citizen population throughout Roman territory. Again, some combination of lesser schools and apprenticeship must be imagined.

Thus, at the level both of practice and of education, we have a similar situation. Nearly all our evidence comes from a limited, elevated stratum of the population. Nonetheless, we must suppose that there was substantial legal activity, both educational and practical, at lower levels. While it is not impossible that much of this lost legal activity paralleled that at the higher levels, we have little reason to assume that that is the case.

7. SOCIAL CONTROL

❦❦❦❦❦❦❦❦

A T ALL TIMES, but especially during the Republic, the Roman government lacked a police force and other bureaucracies that could check ordinary crime, much less control behavior that was less dangerous but still disfavored. Attempts have been made to find elements of the Roman government that might have taken on these functions, but the evidence has been lacking. No magistrate had a major responsibility in this area, nor did any have at his disposal the large number of dedicated employees that would have been required to police a city the size of Rome. In fact, it has recently been pointed out that police forces in general are actually a very recent invention. Rome was somewhat unusual for a premodern state in not allowing military forces into the city, which meant that they could not be used to enforce public order. (Presumably, they would not have been effective for less organized antisocial behavior anyway.) Still, the Romans found ways to try to use law to impose a certain degree of social control.

VIOLENCE

Early Roman law and tradition had, if not encouraged, at least accepted a fair amount of self-help in protecting one's own rights. We know of several forms of more or less ritualized protest and shaming that a wronged party might use to get justice from the supposed wrongdoer: harassing verses, appearing in public in mourning clothes, and simply calling out for aid. Various legal procedures, such as the most basic forms of legal summons and claim to ownership, involved the symbolic enactment of force. Even in the late Republic, disputes over land could be initiated by the symbolic ejection of one party from the disputed land. Now, much of this did not directly involve real violence, but it certainly pointed in that direction. There were also situations and rules that led more directly to the use of force. Defense of one's own person, even in situations not threatening death, was taken to justify use of force in response. Members of the elite, at least, habitually traveled with armed guards, especially outside cities. Even at lower levels of society, ownership of weapons was probably common. There were no real legal restrictions, and many men had done military service. Under certain circumstances, wrongdoers caught in the act (thieves, adulterers) could be killed by the injured party. Bodily injury could be redressed in early law by exacting a parallel injury. Creditors could sometimes recover a debt by directly seizing the debtor's property or even his person. Slaves were subject to arbitrary violence from their owners (Chapter 12), and even attacks on them by others were restricted only if they caused damage to the property or reputation of the owner (Chapter 18).

Over the course of the late Republic and early Empire, however, more and more of this behavior came to be discouraged or even criminalized. *Vis*, a criminal offense that originally encompassed riot and sedition, was extended "downward" to more private, individualized acts of violence (see Chapter 19). Public possession of weapons (at least in the city of Rome) was restricted by laws. At first (around 50 BC) this was on a temporary basis, but the rules were made permanent perhaps a few decades later. Augustus' law on adultery restricted the right of retaliation. Many (though not all) of the traditional forms of self-help became actionable as defamatory (see the next section and Chapter 18). Duress became a reason to void contracts normally enforced without regard for external circumstance (see Chapter 12 on *stricti iuris*) in 80 BC.

The most important antiviolence developments, however, probably surround late second-/early first-century changes in the law of possession. In general, the praetors developed methods known as interdicts to protect possession of property (Chapter 14). There were several of these designed for somewhat different circumstances, but at least two forbid the use of force to recover property. All but one share a common set of exceptions. That is, they would *not* protect your possession of some property from various attacks if you had obtained it yourself by "force, stealth, or [temporary] permission of the owner." The one interdict without these exceptions is also instructive. It is designed to grant recovery of land seized by organized armed force. That is, if no one is entirely innocent, the lesser degree of force is to be preferred. Thus various areas of the law worked together to discourage violence.

DEFAMATION

The earliest Roman law may have provided some protection against defamation, if that is the point of the ban in the Twelve Tables on "evil chants." It seems more likely, however, that that provision was actually directed against magical spells. If so, then there was no known legal defense against defamation until the expansion of *iniuria* law in the mid second century brought it under the same heading as personal injury (Chapter 18). We noted earlier that Roman culture contained a number of standard devices for public insult. These seem generally to have been used by the less powerful against the more power-ful. So, for instance, a man who thought his property had been damaged by a wealthy neighbor's construction might follow that man in the streets, dressed in mourning garb. We know that an *iniuria* action could arise not only from explicit verbal abuse, but also from these more symbolic forms of public sham-ing. In part, the creation of these legal penalties may have been meant to help the already powerful. But there may also be a more broad-minded reason to group all these activities together with physical assault. The activities penalized under the newer scheme were likely to lead to violent situations. American law has occasionally used the notion of "fighting words" (in the context of freedom-of-speech law), that is, language so power-fully shaming or insulting that it is likely to, or inevitably will, lead to violence. There is a community interest in not getting to that point. (It must be admitted, however, that while Roman society placed great weight on personal honor and shame, it seems never to have developed a dueling culture.)

Comparison with the modern law of defamation shows two important gaps in our knowledge of how the Roman law worked. First, in modern American law, truth is an absolute defense to charges of libel and slander. That is, as long as what you say is true, it is irrelevant how insulting your words are or why you uttered them. You cannot have committed libel or slander (though you might conceivably have liability on some other grounds). Did Roman law have such a defense? There is certainly not one written in those terms, and in general Rome lacked the modern commitment to freedom of speech. On the other hand, to constitute *iniuria*, an activity had to be "contrary to good morals." So, for instance, engaging in a certain degree of disrespect to "correct" an ex-slave was considered normal and appropriate, even if the same "correction" applied to a free-born person might spawn a lawsuit. It is possible that the issue of truth could arise in this context, but seemingly not in a decisive way. Second, "public figures" have diminished protections under American law. They have to show that the defamer knew his words were false or disregarded significant evidence to that effect. The goal here is again the protection of free speech in general; application of the regular law of defamation to public figures would create too many incidental impediments to discussion of matters of public importance. Did Roman law have this idea? No, and in fact it might be argued it took the reverse approach. Insult to a high-status individual might be treated as a particularly aggravated form of the offense on the theory that that person had more to lose. It is, however, worth noting a possible gap between theory and practice on this point. The law as written would appear to give elites broad protection, but we know that, at least among the political class, they engaged in fierce, highly personal invective. As far as we know, no one ever filed or even threatened an *iniuria* suit under these circumstances. This may be because the plaintiff was required to feel subjective insult in addition to proving an objective outrage. Perhaps they did not want to give their enemies the satisfaction of publicly admitting their wounds. At any rate, it is worth considering the fact that social custom could play just as big a role as law in social control.

DISGRACE

Socially "deviant" behavior without specific ties to violence was often officially stigmatized instead of being outlawed. The principal legal device here is the notion of *infamia*, "disgrace." This is a formal status (or rather a family of related statuses) imposed on persons involved in various suspect activities. In some cases, this meant members of "lower" professions: actors, gladiators and their trainers, prostitutes and pimps. In others, it meant those who had been convicted of public offences (at least those who were not exiled entirely) or of "delicts" like theft that came near to being crimes. Or it could involve persons who had lost trials in noncriminal cases that nonetheless touched on matters of trustworthiness (such as trusteeship or partnership) or who had been convicted of abuse of legal process (e.g., collusion or false accusation). Finally, it seems to have included some persons who engaged in behavior that was strictly speaking neither illegal nor professional, particularly male homosexuals and dishonorably discharged soldiers. The consequences of *infamia* varied depending on the precise situation, but in general they involved limits on participation in public and legal life: holding office, belonging to the army, membership in the elite "orders," public speaking, representing others, judging, and witnessing in court. Note that these consequences would not be particularly significant on a day-to-day basis for members of the working class, including all the professions that were automatically infamous. This combination officially tied the behavior to the social hierarchy (to which it was broadly correlated in the first place). The "right" people were checked from "deviancy" (justifying their ongoing superior position) while still benefiting from the exploitation of their moral "inferiors."

The Roman census had similar effects, though on a more limited scale. In addition to counting citizens (as in a modern census), the Roman version evaluated them for wealth and (at the top of the wealth scale) for moral correctness. The penalties for a negative evaluation (a censorial "mark") were again civic disabilities that would affect only a tiny fraction of the population. As with the rules of *infamia*, one of the main goals here seems to have been to create the association of social hierarchy with moral hierarchy. And much the same was done by legislation of the emperor Augustus encouraging marriage and procreation and criminalizing adultery. Adulterers and members of infamous professions (like those just listed) could not (re-)marry the free-born.

As just noted, the practical force of the penalties of *infamia* was weak against those of lower status, who were in fact the majority of the population. Similarly, the restrictions on public life had virtually no effect on women, as they were already largely restricted to private life. For these two major groups, *infamia* would be a deterrent only if individuals were genuinely invested in their sense of honor in its own right. In fact, honor as such may have been the central issue even for elite men. There are some dramatic stories of breakdowns in the coercive power of disgrace. In AD 19, a woman named Vistilia registered as a prostitute as a means of escaping penalties for adultery. Since prostitution was legal, it is not surprising that prostitutes were exempt from adultery law. What lawmakers had not foreseen was the "loophole" this created for persons who wished to evade the law by "admitting" falsely to disgraceful behavior. (In the event, she was not allowed to use this strategy, but the principles seem clear). There are also multiple stories of early imperial aristocrats deliberately committing offenses in order to incur *infamia* and thus escape legal restrictions on persons of status. The law tied increased status to increased restrictions on behavior, assuming people would pick status. Mechanisms were lacking for those who picked freedom.

MAINTAINING ORDER

So how did the Romans maintain public order without a large police force or other state apparatus to do so? In part, they may not have. Rome seems to have been, among other things, a more violent place than would be tolerated in a modern Western city. But the lawmaking class was protected by high walls and private security. Also, self-help (whether in forms encouraged by the law or not) may have kept really antisocial behavior in check. Perhaps thefts were discouraged by the threat of vendetta. But to the extent that the provisions of the law just discussed were designed to maintain order, we can perhaps discern two main principles at work. The first is that of exemplarity. When the law did take action, it did so in the most visible way possible. So, for instance, many criminal offenses could be committed only by members of the elite, guaranteeing that most trials would be celebrity trials. The public shaming involved in the censorial mark or *infamia* was designed to "make an example of" the offender. The other principle is mutual surveillance. The lack of any state prosecutor opened criminal prosecution up to everyone (Chapter 19). Rewards were offered to successful prosecutors (citizenship, legal immunities, even cash) to encourage participation. Restrictions on public participation would be enforced by personal enemies seeking advantage in that sphere. In matters touching on inheritance and marriage, alternative heirs would often have reason to bring wrongdoing before the courts. Thus the whole population could pitch in, in place of a small number of full-time specialists (wiki-policing?).

8. LEGAL (IN)EQUALITY

≋≋≋≋≋≋≋≋

THE AMERICAN DECLARATION of Independence asserts that "all men are created equal." Similar ideas have led most modern legal systems to the ideal (not always lived up to) of equal treatment by the law. Roman society, by contrast, took for granted the idea that different people had different value. Consequently, the Roman legal system recognized or created a variety of inequalities. Most of these are described elsewhere in this book (especially in Chapter 10), but a brief summary in one place will be in order. Women were under restrictions that did not apply to men. Younger and younger children had progressively fewer rights. For political reasons, some people were free (including ex-slaves) and some enslaved. Among the free people, different ones were citizens of different communities. All of these distinctions produced different sets of rights. The blind and the deaf were also restricted, as were the "insane." The wealthy had explicit political privileges, though generally not legal ones. Magistrates did have some legal advantages. Starting from the first century AD, there was a more lenient bankruptcy procedure available to "notable" persons. There is even some evidence that the praetor might (sometimes) simply refuse to grant actions against a more powerful person by a less powerful one. But despite all this, Roman law remained surprisingly egalitarian in certain theoretical respects. To simplify the situation slightly, the factors just listed all affect what questions had to be answered in court, but should not affect a trial once under way. That is, although the praetor had to take all these features of status into account in preparing a formula, he could have done so in a way that concealed the status of the parties from the court. (The major exception, of course, is provided by cases in which someone's status is precisely the issue in dispute.) That, at any rate, is how things were supposed to work in theory. But in practice things are not so neat even in modern systems that are much more self-consciously egalitarian. Factors such as race and wealth seem to exert influence on the outcome of at least some trials today. We might, then, reasonably ask whether Roman trials were actually as fair as they were meant to be.

COSTS OF LITIGATION

Successful litigation required expert help, to provide advocacy and perhaps legal knowledge. Experts of both sorts were typically aristocrats, who often worked on a patronage basis. Would-be clients would have opportunities to take advantage of their social position in proportion to their closeness to that same elite. Additionally, and especially in cases where personal ties were weak, money might help get representation. Direct fees for lawyers were, at different times, restricted or outlawed altogether. But in either case, the rules seem to have been evaded or simply ignored. Attested fees range from the stratospheric to the (for ordinary people) merely high, though it is not clear that the lowest available fees are represented in our sources. Still, even if many or most people could have afforded *some* advocate when necessary, the wealthier party to any given case would clearly have much more to choose from. (Lawyers could not sue to recover even legitimate fees; this may have increased the relevance of personal ties.) We know less about the cost of juristic advice, but we may imagine that this worked in roughly the same way as advocacy. Connections and/or money would give advantage.

The costs of outside assistance were in principle optional, or at least negotiable, but some costs were unavoidable. Travel (often to Rome), lodging, and lost income would have been very burdensome for most. The legal process itself, moreover, entailed certain costs and investments. As we will see in Chapter 12, civil procedure relied heavily on giving security. There was little state apparatus to bring someone to court or enforce judgment, so an elaborate system of bail was put in place. (The importance of this is illustrated by the sheer frequency of examples in the documentary evidence [1, 2].) For this purpose, one would have to promise sums of money (often tied to the value of the suit) for nonappearance, or, more commonly, offer a person who would personally commit to paying in your absence. Both would be much easier for the wealthy, who had both the resources and wealthy friends. Moreover, the law specifically allowed notable and wealthy persons to avoid giving security in the first place, on the theory that they were too visible and too liquid to try to avoid the legal process. Additionally, there was the risk of actual financial loss for plaintiffs in some suits. A common form of litigation involved the wager of a symbolic sum of money over the disputed issue; once this was settled, the actual damages were assessed and awarded in a second stage of proceedings. The sum wagered was tied to the actual value of the suit, and while it was symbolic, it was not merely nominal. A working person might well not have been able to risk the loss even if she had a strong case. Moreover, at least in earlier times, the sum had to be deposited in advance in order for the case to proceed. A poor man might not be able to come up with this amount of cash.

CREDIBILITY

In the ordinary course of things, the parties to a suit were also important witnesses, and so their personal credibility came into play at trial. This was particularly important in a society that put such high value on "character" in legal proceedings. This value stemmed from several presuppositions about personality. First, it was assumed that character did not change much, at least over the course of adult life. Second, character was fairly simple. It could be defined generally as good or bad, perhaps with a few more specific tendencies (boldness or timidity, greed or generosity, etc.). Third, this general character was the main determinant of a person's actions. This set of views meant that all parts of a person's life were relevant to evaluating the others, since they all stemmed from the same source. This must have been handy in cases where the Roman lack of record keeping and forensic science offered them little of what we could call evidence, but it seems to have carried over even to cases in which hard evidence did exist.

From the point of view of modern courts, this broad view of character brings in a lot of "irrelevant" material, and creates at least the opportunity for bias, but not in a predictable way. What was its effect in Rome? We have good reason to believe that it would have created systematic advantages for the wealthy and well-born.

In the previous chapter, we noted how the legal notion of disgrace was used to link status and morality. This linkage also appears in ethical thinking outside the law. The "official" theory was that only the independently wealthy were morally trustworthy, because only they could omit financial considerations in making moral judgments. (They might be corrupt for other reasons, of course, but at least they had a chance.) So working for a wage, emblematic of the solid citizen in modern culture, was a cause for suspicion in Rome. Similar arguments were made about underprivileged groups such as women and ex-slaves. Both were reputed to be morally unreliable and underhanded. A more sympathetic account might suggest that both groups had to learn indirection because they were denied official, public authority. Similarly, their dependence (like that of the nonwealthy) was an externally imposed situation.

Nonetheless, elite males preferred to blame the victims. None of these kinds of person – workers, women, ex-slaves – would automatically lose a case, but their position would need more support (advocacy, physical evidence, etc.) than had they been elite males.

It has been suggested that the moral values just discussed were not necessarily widely held. In particular, we do not have much evidence for the views of the various disfavored groups, and we might think it unlikely that they really believed in their own moral inferiority. This is a reasonable view, but not really relevant here. Criminal juries were drawn from the ranks of the well-to-do – free-born men – and members of the elite could ensure this would also happen in their civil cases. Their "common sense" would have led them to be more trusting of persons like themselves.

CORRUPTION

We may get some insight here from two individuals telling us how they would face the moral problems involved. Cicero, in a letter of instruction to his son in the mid first century BC, outlines the responsibilities of a judge presiding over a case in which a friend is a party. Aulus Gellius (mid second century AD) tells a story of an actual case in which he was a judge; this did not involve a personal friend but a person whom he thought had superior "character." Cicero ended up suggesting that the judge could help the friend with matters like scheduling, but could not throw the case altogether. But note that there was no general rule automatically barring the conflict of interest, and the thought of recusing himself from the case entirely seems out of the question. (Formal connections such as kinship or membership in the same fraternity could bar a judge in certain kinds of suits.) Note that the bias involved in selecting judges meant that only the wealthy would benefit from personal connections. Gellius could not find a way to decide his case the way he wanted (i.e., in favor of the "good" man) and so looked for (and found) a way to get out of the whole thing. Such "moral" bias would, as we have noted earlier, tip heavily in favor of the wealthy and powerful. Both writers probably go further in allowing their personal preference to influence decisions than we would allow today. But even more striking is the fact that both do so in idealizing contexts. Cicero is writing philosophical advice, and Gellius is almost smug in describing how he got out of an ethical conundrum. Both are telling their own stories, so they can adjust them for maximum advantage in publicity. They are not "confessing" anything; they are boasting. That suggests that in practice, the level of favoritism in the Roman system must have been quite high.

We have noted already that the Roman courts were weak on mechanisms to compel attendance and obedience to judgments. They seem to have been thought of (at least ideally) as venues for arbitration between more or less willing partners. Between rough equals, this may or may not have worked well, but in circumstances of inequality it would have benefited the stronger party even when no specific favoritism was in play.

For instance, both the initial summons to court and the execution of any eventual judgment required either cooperation by the defendant or some direct application of force by the plaintiff. In the face of an uncooperative defendant, the plaintiff did have some options. More powerful allies might be brought in, whether because of social ties or potential profit. The praetor could impose disgrace or hand out a default judgment (the latter itself needing enforcement). Still, these options might not always be available, and a more powerful party would not need to rely on them in the first place. Even during a trial, the state's hands-off attitude might be relevant. Neither side could legally compel witnesses to testify, nor were there rules against tampering (except by outright bribery). A substantially wealthier or more powerful party would presumably have had a real advantage in attracting witnesses (or in discouraging the other side's witnesses from appearing), even short of paying them.

That possibility leads to a final advantage for the wealthy: bribery. While this was not legal during any period, and became a criminal offense during the late Republic, it may have been common. Accusations of bribery are common in particular cases, but admissions are vanishingly rare (even from positions of relative safety), so it is hard to tell whether most of these supposed instances are just sour grapes. Our credence in these particular cases might be increased by the fact that "money" along with "favoritism" and "power" is one of the stereotypical sources of corruption in political institutions in general, including in the courts. On the other hand, one might argue that the same "myth" could justify both the general and the specific allegations. So, for instance, allegations of "waste and fraud" in government appropriations today are largely self-perpetuating, whatever the facts of any particular case. Even so, one might finally point to the ease of bribery in the Roman world. Judges' identities were known in advance. They were not expected to maintain rigorous segregation from those with business before them. There were no bank or other public financial records of the sort that might be used to prove bribery today. Obviously, if justice can be bought, that helps the wealthy.

9. WRITING AND THE LAW

❧❧❧❧❧❧❧❧

A NCIENT ROME, whether represented today in popular movies or in scholarly books, often looks like a world full of writing. Written texts can outlive their mortal writers, and the effect is multiplied when multiple copies are made of one author's work. And clearly the Romans had a fascination with some forms of writing, such as inscriptions on stone. Yet most scholars agree that the average Roman was poorly or not at all literate. In such a world, it is perhaps not surprising that writing had an important but limited role in the law. The simplest illustration of this is provided by the Edict. The very name of this core set of rules points to the world of speech; the word literally means an order "spoken out" by the magistrate. At the same time, a citizen actually encountering the Edict would almost certainly have come across it in the form of an "album" – a wooden board whitewashed and written on with black ink. To examine the whole of the relationship between writing and the law, however, we will need to consider several different variables. What differences were there between the treatment of the laws proper and that of individual legal instruments (e.g., contracts)? Were all forms or media of writing equivalent?

When did writing have a practical value (as external memory or evidence, for instance), and when did it become part of the law itself? As I suggested earlier, Roman attitudes contain some self-contradiction. Nonetheless, we can see a slow, fairly steady move over time to accept the written word and eventually to privilege it in certain ways over the spoken.

WRITING THE LAWS

For the Romans themselves, the greatest moments in legal history were occasions of writing down, and the most important was the publication of the original legal code, the Twelve Tables, in about 450 BC. The surviving fragments are some of our earliest direct sources of information on Rome. Ancient accounts tend to see the Tables as a populist measure, since they limited the ability of the elite to apply the law arbitrarily; some today see the reverse, since their publication would have given a gloss of "objectivity" to rules composed by and (largely) for elites. Both views may well be correct. At any rate, the key points here are that (1) the composition (or perhaps mostly collection) of the Tables required a total replacement of the earlier form of Roman government by a special commission for two years, (2) the Tables make up the longest Latin text we know of until more than 200 years later, and (3) even more than three centuries later, schoolboys were still learning the Tables as the heart of the legal system. At least in the establishment of law, the influence of writing was crucial and lasting from almost the earliest times. Similar, though of less importance, was the publication of a collection of *legis actiones* by Gnaeus Flavius in 312 BC. These special formulas were required to take a matter to court and thus to give practical effect to the rights theoretically offered by the laws (Chapter 11).

The Twelve Tables were preserved by generations of copying, for patriotic as well as for legal reasons. When we start to see evidence for more "ordinary" law (mid second century BC, though our sources only start then), we see that it has a built-in concern with writing. That is, a standard clause at the end of the text of many laws ordered that they be posted in a place where they could be read easily from ground level. Now, such a clause may not always have been included (and perhaps laws without it would be less likely to survive for us to read), but it is common enough, and the wording standardized enough, to suggest that it was the norm. "Publication" of this sort is not quite like what happens today. These laws ordinarily seem to require that only one copy of themselves be set up. This also seems to have been the situation with the album of the praetor's Edict. Someone who wanted to know what was in one of these laws would have to find (and potentially travel to) the location where it was set up and copy it himself, or have this done, or in rare cases get access to circulating manuscript copies of some particularly important texts. We have already noted (Chapter 4) the weakness of the Roman archiving laws.

The kinds of writing just described go back to the very early history of Roman law and government. Two other forms developed later, extending the importance of the written word. The first to arise were the various writings of the jurists (Chapter 5). The crucial transition seems to have been from the giving of oral answers in consultation (*responsa*) to the collection and publication of these responses. This is first attested around 200 BC, though it may have begun earlier. From there it was relatively easy to move to commentaries and treatises with more abstract structure. Surviving juristic writing often cites other jurists, even across large swaths of time, indicating the fundamentally writing-based nature of their project. Written from the beginning, moreover, was the form of Imperial legislation known as the "rescript." This took the form of an emperor's response to a petition (itself a written text), written at the end of the original petition document itself and returned. Some of these will have been of interest only to the parties immediately concerned, but others became precedents of great generality. Much of Roman government operated on this petition-and-response model, so many rescripts are not sources of law in a straightforward sense. Still, the rescript was the standard mechanism for dealing with judicial appeals to the emperor, and so it became an important (and necessarily written) source of law.

It is worth noting how closely the rescript is tied to the actual physical petition. Nothing about the process requires the existence of more than a copy for the petitioner (and, generally, one in the imperial files). In some cases, interested parties would post the text of rescripts in more lasting materials. In others, the texts made their way into the juristic tradition and so could be copied repeatedly in manuscript. Both cases illustrate a more general point about the use of writing in making law. Writing was clearly a normal part of fixing the law, and probably at some point became a necessary one. On the other hand, there was no general provision for the use of writing to publicize the contents of those laws.

DOCUMENTS AND SAYINGS

The role of documents in individual cases is a more complicated matter, but in general we can say that it was less important than in the making of laws. In some respects, legal proceedings were expected to be oral, in others written, and yet in other ways the issue is more complex. In this section we will look at the use of "legal documents" (in a narrow sense) and the use of oral "sayings" in their place. By the former, I mean the kind of documents produced specifically because the law required them as part of some larger legal process. A written will would be an example of this in both common and Roman law. I will use the term "saying" to mean some set of words with a similar function, but uttered aloud. Oaths are typically sayings of this sort in either system (noted, in written form, in [9, 12]). In the next section, we will look at documents and sayings in a broader sense – that is, the way the legal system used written or oral expressions that had not been created originally, or at least not exclusively, for the purposes of the law.

The most general feature of trials that emphasizes orality is the restriction of the deaf from pleading in court. (This is a procedural issue, not a substantive one; all their legal rights could be upheld by an advocate.) "For," the jurist Ulpian explains, "no one was to be allowed to make application who was unable to hear the praetor's decision." Key parts of the trial literally did not exist in written form – or perhaps this was an agreed-on fiction. In either case, the importance of the spoken word is highlighted. A somewhat more specific legal device shows a similar radical prejudice in favor of orality. One of the most important forms of Roman contract was the so-called *stipulatio* (Chapter 12). This contract was entered into when one party asked whether the other swore to carry out certain actions (almost any legal act could be promised), and the second party replied that he did. This seems odd to many moderns. When we require certain kinds of formality (e.g., signing a contract), those forms tend to be self-proving. The formalities of *stipulatio* (the use of certain words for "swear," the oral question and answer) are complete failures on this ground. On independent grounds we can assume that *stipulatio* goes back to the earliest days of Roman law, and so presumably to a day when any requirement for writing would be unlikely or impossible. More importantly for the present issue, later Romans preserved the form even when it was no longer necessary. This retention presumed and reinforced the idea that, at least in theory, some legal transactions might be purely oral. (The facts are a little more complicated than this, and we will return to *stipulatio* later.)

There are a slightly larger number of contexts in which Roman law *required* writing compared to those in which it was not acceptable, but only one of these is of much importance.

That main usage is, not surprisingly, for the making of wills (Chapter 16). In theory, these could have been composed orally (like a *stipulatio*), but not only would this create serious evidentiary problems, it would remove the possibility of confidential wills, which Romans seem to have found desirable. There was also a form of contract (called *litteris*, "by letters") that was entered into by creating certain entries in account books under appropriate circumstances. The details are obscure, but such contracts seem to have been fairly rare. These two devices are Republican, but other legal uses of writing developed over the course of the Empire. Augustan legislation allowed for registration of births and wills. The emperor Constantine required a number of private transactions (e.g., sale of land) to be registered to guarantee their effect. And even more directly, he required that gifts be effected by written documents. (These requirements were rolled back by later emperors.)

DOCUMENTS IN LEGAL PROCEEDINGS

These extreme cases, in which writing was either required or unacceptable, however, are relatively few. Much of what went on in Roman law could proceed either with or without written documents. For instance, the "consensual" contracts (Chapter 12) could be written down or not, as could notice of intent to sue. This means that the line between "legal documents" in the narrow sense and documents that just happened to be used in court was somewhat fuzzy. To see why, let us consider a specific kind of transaction – say, the sale of a book. Sale was one of the consensual contracts, meaning (among other things) that it was created by the mere fact of agreement between the buyer and seller. Writing was not required, nor was it binding if there had not actually been agreement. Still, the existence of a written document might be very convincing to a court that had to decide what agreement, if any, had been entered into by the parties. Conversely, the absence of any documentation may have seemed suspicious, even if it did not automatically end a case. In modern terms, a written contract of this sort was not "constitutive" (it did not bind anyone by itself), but it did have an evidentiary function. This is different from the (rare) contract *litteris* discussed earlier, in which the writing was constitutive of the contract. In the case of sale and the other consensual contracts, a written document served an evidentiary role closer to that of, say, accounting records. My cancelled check does not absolutely settle the question of whether you agreed to sell me a book at a given price, or even if I paid that price (the check could have been for something else), but it might help persuade a court of both points.

The value of particular documents for proving particular points must have varied enormously from case to case, but we can note four features that illustrate the conflicts particularly well. The first has to do with how lawyers were trained to deal with documents, the second with redundant witness testimony, the third with real-world complications of *stipulatio* (the contract whose theory we just discussed), and the fourth with a particular form of writing that was important for legal activities.

Roman legal sources have very little to say specifically about the value of writing as evidence. Most of the few texts just point out that it is rarely necessary, though there might be an implication that it is generally better to have documents on your side. The question seems, however, to have been of much more interest to the rhetoricians – professors of public speaking whose central focus was training young men to speak in the courts. We have many rhetorical handbooks, and they all explain in general terms how an advocate should handle documentary evidence and oral testimony. Ignoring the detail, we can note simply that any lawyer would have been able to argue for or against the value of either, depending on what was more useful for his side. Some have argued that this advice shows a slight preference for written evidence, but the clearer and more important point is that speakers were prepared for either.

A specific kind of evidence that might come into play could be something called today by the Latin name of *testatio*. This is not a pre-existing document like a contract or file called into the proceedings, nor is it a part of the legal proceeding itself, like a summons to court. Rather, it is a statement or affidavit, recording someone's testimony and introduced by one of the parties. In some cases, this kind of document had an obvious practical value. A faraway witness, or simply one who did not wish to appear in public, could not be compelled to appear but might be willing to put his or her words in writing. It also seems to have been common enough for corporate bodies to use such written statements; after all, a defendant's hometown could not literally appear on the stand to attest to his good character, but the city council could approve a written statement. What is perhaps surprising, then, is that we know of many cases in which witnesses who were physically present and testifying also provided *testationes*. Some of these cases may technically involve a distinction between live testimony by individuals and a written *testatio* from an organization to which they belonged, but this is not always the case. This suggests that the mere fact of documentary form may have lent extra credibility to what could otherwise have been expressed orally.

Similarly, the actual practice of making *stipulatio* contracts may show that the public was more convinced than the legal system of the value of writing agreements down. This kind of contract had, as we have noted, a required oral component, but it seems to have had no written one. It is striking, then, that so many of the written legal instruments we have are in fact stipulations [1, 2, 4, 8–10, 12]. In fact, it has even been claimed that the contract actually did have an obligatory written component not mentioned by any legal sources. This seems unlikely, but it does point out the seeming mismatch of our evidence for theory and practice. However, a better explanation might be along the lines just suggested for *testationes*. Real individuals without (or despite) professional legal knowledge of the irrelevance of writing seem to have felt that it conveyed extra certainty to the proceedings. This may have been for more or less practical reasons; documents have a clearer and impartial memory. It may also have been for more "magical" reasons; especially in a world where illiteracy was the norm, the mere fact of writing may have given the written words special power. Likely, both were true to some extent.

This quasi-magical effect may also be the explanation for another phenomenon. Romans seem to have had a preference for certain media of writing above and beyond their practical advantages. For laws and similar permanent, public documents, bronze seems to have been the preferred medium. For private documents, special importance seems to have been given to wax tablets. These were sheets of wood with a raised border that enclosed a surface of wax. The wax was written on by carving into it with a pointed object and could be erased by being smoothed over.

10. STATUS

I N CERTAIN RESPECTS, Roman law could be surprisingly
egalitarian. Once a case came to trial, particularly, the court
was supposed to decide between one case and the other, not
one person and the other (at least in theory; for the practice, see
Chapter 7). Still, Roman society was one in which it could be
openly asserted that some people were simply better than others, and the law recognized some of these hierarchies (e.g., free
persons vs. slaves). Other status differences might be claimed
to exist in natural fact (minors vs. full adults) or on political
rather than personal grounds (e.g., citizenship). The most complex and important of these issues have to do with gender, and
the position of women in Roman law will get its own chapter
(Chapter 16). This chapter will treat all the other distinctions of
status just mentioned.

FREEDOM AND SLAVERY

Many societies have some form or another of "involun-
tary servitude" (as the American Constitution describes it)

or compulsory labor. Rome (in common with the American South) had the rarer and stronger institution of "chattel" slavery. That is, not only were some human beings compelled to labor or follow the orders of others, but they were actually subject to the laws that governed property of other types. In principle, parts of the law of persons could have been applied at the same time. In fact, as we will see, the "thing"ness of Roman slaves stayed constant over the centuries, but their "person"ness varied. Before turning to the details of the legal situation, it will be helpful to say a few words about the broader historical context, and in particular to note some differences from the kind of slavery more familiar to us from American history. The original ancient slaves were captives taken in war. The slaves taken in Rome's earliest wars would have been ethnically and linguistically similar to their new owners. As the empire grew and new captives became more obviously "foreign," they came from across the Mediterranean basin and did not necessarily resemble one another. Some even came from places (say, Greece) with more "high culture" than Rome and were recognized for it. You might even buy a skilled tutor for your children. Moreover, for reasons to be noted, many of these slaves and/or their descendants were eventually integrated into the citizen body. Thus, while no one in Rome seems ever to have questioned the general idea of slavery, it lacked the kind of racial or other "natural" basis claimed for it in the modern American case. Slavery was usually recognized as a matter of individual (mis)fortune.

While perhaps less pernicious in this overall sense, Roman slavery does not seem to have been much better from the point of view of the individual slave. Slaves were fully property and so were subject to whatever use and abuse their owners wished, including hard labor, sexual exploitation, torture, and summary execution. Less dramatically, slaves were potential objects of commerce, so they could be bought and sold away from their families and friends without recourse or even warning. While lucky slaves could in practice control or at least make use of considerable wealth (see the last section of this chapter for details), they could never be its legal owner or possessor, and so they could lose everything at any time at their owner's whim.

Since there was no racial or other class "naturally" equated with slavery, slaves could be released by their owners. This is called manumission. It might be a reward for good service, a show of generosity, or just an easy way to cut expenses in lean times. Manumission was a common event, though the average individual's chances of being freed were probably not good. Not only did manumitted slaves cease to be the property of their owners, but they ceased to be property at all. Furthermore, they became Roman citizens (see the next section on citizenship). This is striking both because it shows an interesting degree of openness to (former) slaves in Roman society and because it is one of the few cases in Roman law where a private act (manumission) is allowed to affect a normally public category (citizenship). Originally, there were no limits on manumission other than the interests of the owner. It might be carried out during the owner's lifetime or (quite commonly) by her will. The emperor Augustus introduced restrictions on the number and age of slaves manumitted (and on the age of the person doing the manumitting), but the basic procedure remained the same. A former slave is called a "freedman" (note the "d"); the former owner is called a "patron." The freedman had a social duty of continued deference to the patron, and often a legal duty to continue to provide some labor (the details were negotiated at the time of manumission). The patron also had some rights to inherit from the freedman. The freedperson had no rights "upward" against the patron, but might in practice be treated as a member of the family, especially in common burial [20, 21]. A freedperson had limited rights in public law (e.g., no office holding) but was an almost entirely normal citizen in private law. The freedperson's free-born child was a full Roman in both respects. Note, however, that the freedperson's life as a legal person effectively began at the time of manumission. Any children or other "family" they might have had beforehand was not legally connected to them. So, for instance, freeing a slave would not, by itself, free his children from the same owner. And even if they were freed at the same time, they would not (from the point of view of the law) be their father's "children."

Originally slaves did not have the kind of civil or criminal liability that free persons did. If a slave was accused by a private citizen of damaging property (or committing some other delict; see Chapter 18), she could not be sued by the normal procedure. Instead, the owner of the slave had two choices.

Either she could assume the potential liability herself (and be tried for the slave's actions), or she could surrender the slave to the aggrieved party to do with as he wished. (What they actually did – torture? execution? resale? hard labor? – is unclear.) This latter option is called "noxal surrender." Slaves accused of "public" (i.e., criminal) offenses were apparently dealt with summarily by magistrates. Over the course of the empire, direct trials of slaves for criminal offenses were introduced, but noxal surrender remained the norm for civil actions.

CITIZENSHIP

Citizenship is a particularly important status category because Roman law (like most ancient systems) was primarily "personal" rather than "territorial" in its reach. That is, "Roman law" was not thought of as the law of a particular area, but law for Roman people, wherever they happened to be. (Note that this does not mean that foreigners in Rome were unconstrained by the law. It would be more accurate to say that they were largely unprotected by the law, both against individuals and against the state.) Citizenship was typically inherited from one's parents. If they had different citizenships, or if they were not legally married, then the children normally inherited their mother's status. There was no normal method of naturalization, though citizenship could be given as a reward for service to the Roman state. The main sources of new citizens were manumission of individual slaves (as just discussed) and imperial grants to whole cities or provinces between the mid first century AD and 212, when all free persons in the empire were made citizens (Chapter 2). Initially, the main distinction was between citizens of Rome (*cives*) and everyone else (*peregrini*). From time to time political circumstances led to the creation of various intermediate categories. Most important were the "Latins," a group whose precise definition and membership changed a great deal over time, but who can be thought of in all periods as partial Roman citizens.

The earliest Roman law followed the personality principle rigorously, and that rule continued to have force much longer in some areas of the law. Thus, for instance, the whole of procedure by *legis actio* (Chapter 11) was limited to citizens, as were the formal modes of transferring ownership (Chapter 13). Marriages were recognized only between Roman citizens, and wills could be made only by citizens for the benefit of Roman citizens. (Romans would not claim that only their fellow citizens were married or left wills, only that Roman justice was not entitled to pass judgment on the cases of *peregrini*.) Other areas of the law, particularly those clearly governed by the Edict, were available to anyone. The law of consensual contracts is the most prominent example, but even in other areas the praetor eventually introduced other devices to bring in noncitizens. Moreover, Latins and other privileged groups were given access to Roman marriage law (*conubium*) and/or commercial law (*commercium*).

STATUSES OF THE FREE

Among free Roman citizens there were a number of distinctions of rank. For instance, throughout the Republic there were status groups ("orders") of "knights" (wealthy and of free descent) and "senators" (knights who had started a political career) at the top of society. Smaller towns outside Rome often had similar orders on a local scale. Members of the elite had special protection from defamation (Chapter 18). These distinctions, however, were mostly of social and political importance; they did not much affect the kinds of legal issues discussed in this book (at least in theory). Of more importance was a distinction that evolved primarily in the second century AD. Roman criminal law of the Republic had strongly avoided corporal punishment for Roman citizens (Chapter 19). Slaves and foreigners were subject to anything the authorities could imagine. Over the course of the early Empire (and, perhaps not accidentally, at a time when the proportion of persons who were citizens was on the rise), the privilege of avoiding torture and execution was restricted to a more select group. Those who more or less retained the old privilege were the *honestiores* ("more honorable"), while the newly vulnerable masses were dubbed *humiliores* ("more humble"). The dividing line seems to have fallen roughly at the level of the municipal orders. Not just the Roman elite, but that of the towns were *honestiores*; all the rest were *humiliores*.

AGE

In most societies a person does not have full (or perhaps any) legal rights until reaching some age of adulthood. In some cases there are different ages for different purposes, say, eighteen for voting and control of one's own property in the United States and England, slightly younger to be able to drive, and slightly older in the United States to buy alcohol. Roman law observed a number of such distinctions (to be discussed shortly), but the most important marker of adulthood was not tied to a specific age. A Roman could not own any property or perform any binding transactions, regardless of age, as long as his or her father was still alive. Any property that might happen to come into the child's hands became the property of the father. (This is one reason inheritance law was so important to the Romans.) More generally, the authority of a father over his children, of whatever age, was supposedly absolute. Our sources even insist on his right to execute them at will, though actual instances are so rare that some have questioned the rule itself. The theoretical power was restricted in the second century AD and abolished by the emperor Constantine. Interestingly, this dramatic hierarchy did not affect the public sphere. A qualified citizen could be elected to public office whether or not his father was still alive. He would still not, however, have any property to his name.

A NOTE ON TERMINOLOGY: There are several important and often similar-sounding Latin terms in this area of the law, and it may be helpful to set them out together. A father's authority over his children is called *patria potestas*, "fatherly power"; the state of being under this authority is being *in potestate*, "in power"; and the state of not being in power is being *sui iuris*, "in one's own power." A male who is not in power is also called a *pater familias*, "father of the family," even if he has no children and even if he is a child in years. Children in power (of whatever age) are called *filius/filia familias*, "son/daughter of the family."

Absent a living father, the law made several distinctions based on age. Children younger than seven were by rule incapable of forming intentions, which meant (among other things) that they could not make contracts or be liable for criminal activity. They might own property, but it would largely be in the hands of a guardian (*tutor*). The guardian could carry out transactions in the child's name, though he was required to act in his or her best interests and to give security as a guarantee. (When old enough, the child could sue to guarantee that the guardian had done his job [26].) Depending on circumstances, the guardian might be named in the father's will, picked from near relatives (the "nearest agnate," as in intestate inheritance; see Chapter 15), or in the last instance named by a magistrate. Children older than this, but younger than twelve (for girls) or fourteen (for boys), still had the same kind of guardian, but could form intentions. In principle, they could make binding agreements, though these had to be ratified by the guardian. These ages were picked as the typical minimum at which a person might produce heirs of his or her own. It is at this point, the Romans seem to think, that a person was fully vested in his or her own property; before this age, there was still a sense that it might revert to the broader family. Finally, up to the age of twenty-five, a person might plead youth and inexperience in order to have a transaction invalidated if he came to have second thoughts. Such restitution was not automatic, and could be blocked in advance by the appointment of a sort of pseudo-guardian (*curator*) to monitor the young person's transactions.

INSANITY

The law also created forms of guardianship for two related classes of persons: the insane and the spendthrift. For these purposes, the "insane" must have meant people who had substantially lost touch with reality. Like the youngest children, they could not, as a matter of law, form intents and so were prohibited from virtually any legal activity, including commercial transactions, marriage, testimony in court, and even conviction for crimes. The "spendthrift" were merely reckless with their (inherited?) property and accordingly were less constrained. They were prevented only from alienating property without approval from the guardian. Normally, family members would have sought the designation of the insane or spendthrift person, and an (agnatic) family member often served as guardian. Judicial officials, however, could make the decision on their own and could appoint someone they thought would be more trustworthy. What the standards were for placing or revoking either designation, we do not know. The law does, however, seem to assume that at least some people will slip in and out of these states, and that their legal situation should fluctuate accordingly.

PECULIUM AND AGENCY

It has often been noted that the legal positions of slaves and children in power were quite similar. One institution that applies in both cases is a kind of fund called *peculium*. Neither group could technically own property, but it was often found to be convenient to allow them to operate as if they did – say, in running a partially independent business. This pseudo-property could include cash or any other property (including slaves, who could then be virtually owned by other slaves! [8]). A slave operating a business would presumably be expected to keep it running in the black after the initial investment; a grown son or daughter of the political class might be given a more regular allowance just for support. Anything that was earned by the use of the *peculium* was typically funneled back in (or at least some percentage, as informally agreed between the father/owner and child/slave). To make this legally sound, the praetor allowed someone who did business with the child or slave to sue the father or owner for up to the value of the *peculium* (at the time of the original deal) to enforce their agreements.

Slaves and children were also useful to help fill a gap in Roman commercial law. Roman law had little in the way of agency. That is, only the actual parties to a transaction had any obligations from it; contrast buying, say, computer software at a store today, where the warranties and other obligations lie with Microsoft, not with the cashier. Moreover, Roman law did not recognize the "artificial persons" we call corporations. Today I buy software from Microsoft, not from Bill Gates personally. This was impossible in Rome. Children and slaves provide a partial exception, since they can make acquisitions for their father/owner. Their use as extensions was limited because they still had a limited capacity to undertake obligations for him. (See Chapter 12 on *societas* and Chapter 14 on joint ownership for other aspects of the "corporation" issue.)

11. CIVIL PROCEDURE

꘎꘎꘎꘎꘎꘎꘎꘎

I F SOMEONE SAYS the word "law" to you, the first things likely to come to your mind will include "courts" and "trials." Arguably, that is a distorting view, and the law has its greatest effect less directly – when people know how to follow the rules on their own without direct enforcement or judgment, as in a game of pick-up football. Still, even that situation probably could not exist without at least the possibility of formal trials, and courts are one of the most distinctive features of what we would recognize as a "legal" system. This chapter will discuss the procedure in what we usually call Rome's "civil" courts (the actual Latin word is "private"), where the vast majority of cases were heard. Criminal (literally "public") procedure will be treated in Chapter 19. I will begin by discussing the set of rules used during most of our period: the so-called formulary procedure. Then I will treat more briefly its predecessor (the *legis actiones*) and a partial successor (called *cognitio*).

While this chapter is about procedural rules, not the substantive law discussed in most of the rest of this book, I should make one substantive point here. Since the civil and criminal courts operated under very different rules, I need to give a very brief description of the different jurisdictions here. The civil courts handled not only most of the matters that their American and British counterparts do – like contracts, property damage, and inheritance – but also most forms of theft and most crimes of violence. Thus the rules given in this chapter have a particularly broad relevance.

FORMULARY PROCEDURE

This way of arranging cases gets its name from the *formula*, an instruction given to the judge(s) hearing the case on how they should go about deciding it. The origins of the procedure are unclear. It arose perhaps around 150 BC, and may or may not have been introduced all at once. Formulary trials fell into two quite distinct phases. The first of these (called *in iure*, "at law") was a kind of preliminary hearing in which the parties consulted with an elected magistrate to set up the ground rules for a hearing on their specific problem [3]. Then came the trial proper, called the *apud iudicem* ("before a judge") phase. Here there were arguments and the presentation of evidence and witnesses. At the end, the judge (in some cases a panel of judges) delivered a verdict.

The official in charge of the first, *in iure* phase was ordinarily the urban praetor. This office was part of the standard ladder that ambitious politicians had to climb if they wanted to reach the highest positions (Chapter 2). Thus any given praetor would always have been an aristocrat and a politician, but would not necessarily be a legal specialist. The praetor's job was to arrange for a judge (*iudex*) and to produce directions to that judge (the *formula*). The formula specified (a) the identity of the parties; (b) the basic question to be decided (the *intentio*); (c) special defenses, responses to these, responses to the responses, and so on; and (d) the stakes to be decided. The following is a fairly full formula (see also [26]):

> Let Titius be appointed judge. If it appears that Aulus Agerius deposited a silver table with Numerius Negidius and that the same was not returned to Aulus Agerius by the bad faith of Numerius Negidius, let the judge condemn Numerius Negidius to pay the value of the matter to Aulus Agerius. If it does not so appear, absolve him.

(Aulus Agerius and Numerius Negidius are standard placeholder names for the plaintiff and defendant, respectively, in Roman law texts, something like the Latin equivalent of John Doe and Richard Roe. Titius serves similarly for the judge.) Many of the defenses and responses were standard ones that could be cut and pasted together with a variety of different kinds of *intentio*. So, for instance, the *intentio* would be slightly different depending on whether a case involved a sale or a rental, but the exception that would allow you to get out of a contract made under duress would be the same for both. The stakes were generally defined in terms of monetary damages, and, depending on the issue of the case, the praetor might specify a precise amount, set an upper limit, or leave the value to the judge's discretion. Finally, one or both parties might be required to put up security (like bail in modern criminal cases) to guarantee their appearance in court.

Three important features of the formula can be noted immediately. First, the praetor does nothing to decide which side is right. Rather, he is trying to extract the legally relevant details of both sides' positions and put them into a single instruction. Second, the terms of the formula are much more general than in a modern charge to a jury. (The example just given is quite typical.) This could give a certain amount of discretion to the trial court, but its main effect was to empower the jurists who "interpreted" the formulas. Finally, while the formula would typically be constructed from elements in the Edict, the praetor could in theory make up a novel one on the spot, especially if a genuinely new situation arose.

The judge who actually heard and decided the case was neither an elected official (like the praetor) nor a legal professional (like most American judges). A single judge was the norm in most cases, though if certain issues were at stake (certain inheritance questions, for instance), multiple judges (called *recuperatores* or *centumviri*) heard the case and decided it by majority vote. In the rest of this chapter I will speak only of the single-judge procedure, since the rules were otherwise the same. The judge could be chosen in different ways. The praetor had a list of adult men who met the qualifications to serve, and the parties could take turns rejecting potential judges they did not want. These qualifications included wealth, free birth and Roman citizenship, and "good character." Whoever was left became the *iudex*. Or, if the parties could agree on a judge in advance, the praetor could simply appoint that person, avoiding the whole rejection process. (In this case, most of the qualifications just mentioned seem to have been waived, though this is not entirely clear, and women and slaves were still out.)

In a typical common law trial, there is a division of labor between a jury, which, if it is used at all, is meant to decide factual questions ("Did he do it?" "What was the deceased cow originally worth?"), and the judge, who answers questions of law ("Does intention need to be proved to convict of murder?" "Can certain kinds of evidence even be mentioned at trial?"). In a Roman trial, the praetor's formula limited the questions of law to be addressed at trial, but the *iudex*, as a practical matter, decided both kinds of questions. Moreover, as we shall see, the set of "questions of law" was rather different then.

Both sides were typically represented by advocates and perhaps also by legal experts (where available; see Chapter 4 on the division of legal professions). Moreover, the *iudex* himself might seek outside legal advice. The procedure was highly adversarial; that is, the court acted as time keeper and ultimate decision maker, but it did almost nothing to help or constrain either sides in the service of "truth." The plaintiff began by making a fairly long speech laying out his case, the defense spoke in opposition, and then the sides in turn presented whatever evidence and witnesses they had gathered. Neither side could subpoena witnesses or "discover" material in the hands of the other side. There were no objections to forms of evidence or argument during the presentations. In principle, this allowed for a lot of irrelevant rhetoric and personal attacks, though it would not help your case if you left the *iudex* thinking you were wasting time.

Once the *iudex* had decided the case, there were no "higher" courts to appeal to, so his decision was final.

The system as a whole seems to have been designed to work best as a state-sponsored form of arbitration. That is, it assumes a certain level of cooperation from both parties to resolve their dispute and a basic agreement that the mechanism is a legitimate one. For instance, the mechanisms to compel the defendant to appear in court in the first place or to execute a judgment at the end of the case were clumsy. Ultimately, the praetor could force cooperation, if nothing else worked, by granting a default judgment and backing it up by allowing the plaintiff to collect by auctioning off the defendant's property. Things worked much better if both parties preferred just to settle the issue by appealing to a neutral third party and move on. Less dramatically, the system of constructing formulas lets both sides tell their story without having to settle any disputes up front, and the selection of the judge is easier if the two parties can reach agreement. So even when compulsion was an option, the system made good use of cooperation.

LEGIS ACTIONES

The formulary procedure was the main one used during the period covered by this book, but it was not the only one. For instance, there was also an earlier procedure involving a so-called *legis actio* ("action at law"), which was largely replaced, but not entirely abolished. From a modern point of view, the outlines of a trial under the *legis actio* procedure were broadly similar to those of a formulary trial. The main difference lay in the formality of the *in iure* proceedings. Instead of hearing both sides and composing a (relatively novel) *formula*, the praetor and the parties followed specified scripts using fixed phrases. Each of these phrases was designed to be used in a specific circumstance. (In English we would probably describe them as "formulaic," if that did not run the danger of confusion with the Latin term for the later type of instruction.) A case could not be brought if it could not be expressed in one or another of these fixed phrases, and even a legitimate cause would fail if those words were spoken incorrectly. These scripts fell into several general forms, but the most important one took the form of a bet backed up by an oath on the matter at issue.

The changeover to the formulary system is not well understood. It is generally thought to have occurred around 150 BC and probably did not happen all at once. Formulas were certainly introduced around that time, but it is not clear when (if at all) any parts of the *legis actio* procedure were formally abolished (as opposed to simply ignored). We do know that as late as the middle of the second century AD *legis actiones* were still occasionally used in special circumstances.

COGNITIO

Over the course of the Empire, a third and more distinct system arose and eventually displaced the formulary system. Today this is generally called *cognitio*; the term is a Latin word for "inquiry, inquisition," and it perhaps did not have quite as specific a technical sense at the time. Under this procedure, the distinction between *in iure* and *apud iudicem* hearings was eliminated. Instead, the same government official organized the case, heard the arguments, and rendered judgment. The identity of the official(s) involved varied over time as the structure of the imperial government evolved. Originally, it might be a praetor or even a consul (at least in hearings on certain topics), but the system did not really take off until they were replaced by new officials created by and answerable to the emperor. At any rate, this official not only combined the old roles of the magistrate and *iudex*, but also could (if he wished) take a more active interest in a given case than either had under the old system – for instance, questioning the parties on his own initiative. Also, in complicated cases, issues could be decided one at a time, rather than trying to resolve a complicated formula all at once. Conversely, issues that arose only in mid-trial could be taken into account, since the judge was not bound by a formula composed beforehand.

During some periods officials authorized to exercise jurisdiction might themselves appoint deputies to hear cases, and in any case always operated as subordinates of the emperor. The existence of a hierarchy created the possibility for appeal that had not existed under either of the earlier systems. In principle, a case could go all the way to the emperor, and his responses to such cases would become a significant source of law. Appeals typically only went up the ladder, unlike those in modern systems, where a higher court often returns a case to a lower one with instructions to reconsider some specific issue.

Procedures of this general sort seem already to have existed during the Republic in the provinces, where Roman governors (essentially military governors) could impose them on noncitizen subjects. Under the empire they quickly became normal in that context, and also started to be used in Rome for cases involving newly formalized legal institutions, such as the *fidei-commissum* (a trust created by will; see Chapter 15). By perhaps the mid third century AD, however, the new procedure seems to have become the dominant one even for old areas of the law.

12. CONTRACTS

〰〰〰〰〰

A "CONTRACT" can be defined roughly as an agreement that can be enforced by the courts or other governmental mechanisms. Roman and Anglo-American law share this notion so far as it goes. An obvious question, however, is how to tell which agreements rise to the level of contracts. In common law, this is a fairly simple issue in principle. Roughly, any seriously intended "agreement, upon a sufficient consideration, to do or not to do a particular thing" counts. "Consideration" here means simply the thing(s) you get in return for fulfilling the agreement. In Roman law, things are more complicated. To be legally enforceable, an agreement had to meet the description of one of several pre-defined *types* of contract. There were more than ten types, and these were in turn divided into groups in different ways (e.g., on the basis of who was under obligation or how the agreement was to be interpreted). In the rest of this chapter I will simplify the situation by treating only five of the most important types of contract.

The most important distinction is between contracts defined by their formalities, on the one hand, and by their content, on the other. Formalities are special words or actions that might be required in the making of a contract, such as writing down an agreement, signing that agreement, shaking hands, registration in some central archive, or even using the word "contract." The one "formal" contract (that is, contract defined by its formalities) to be discussed here is one usually called by its Latin name, *stipulatio* (plural *stipulationes*), which can be roughly translated as "binding promise" (see Chapter 9; [1, 2, 4, 8–10, 12]). The required form was an oral question and answer between the two parties of the form "Do you promise that X?"; "I promise (that X)." Under some circumstances, a particular Latin word for "promise" was required; the long form of the answer seems to have been optional, as long as the verb of the question was repeated. A problem with this form is that it is not self-proving. Unlike, say, signing a contract, there is nothing in the process that automatically provides evidence that the contract was actually agreed to. We will return to this problem later. While the form was to this extent fixed, the content was not. Any promise that was not by nature illegal or impossible became binding when put in these terms.

Most of the other contracts to be discussed here are of a sort called "consensual." They required no particular form in order to come into effect; the mere agreement (Latin *consensus*) of the parties made the contract. They were, however, restricted in terms of substance. Three contracts covered situations of: sale, renting/hiring, and partnership. A consensual agreement that did not fall into one of these areas (or a few others not discussed here) was not a contract at all. So, for instance, a consensual contract could protect sale of a thing for cash, but not trading it for another thing. That does not, of course, mean that barter was illegal; rather, one had to protect it by *stipula-tio* or run the risk of being unable to enforce the agreement in court. Depending on the general category of contract (e.g., formal or consensual) and the particular type within one of these categories (e.g., sale or rental or partnership), certain terms would have to be put into the agreement, others terms could not be put in, and still others would be assumed to be part of the agreement unless something contrary was specified. In the rest of this chapter I will be discussing the specifics of those properties, but it is important to point out here that these are a framework. Beyond the basic agreement, the parties could also include virtually any terms (a "pact") they wished so long as those terms were not somewhere explicitly forbidden [8, 12, 14].

As the question-and-answer form of the *stipulatio* suggests, only the person making the promise was obligated to any future action. This made it what is called a "unilateral" or one-sided contract. (Why would anyone want to make such a promise? In practice, these *stipulationes* often came in pairs and/or included conditions based on what the nonpromising party might do in the future.) The rule for unilateral contracts of this kind was that they were to be judged on a "strict law" (*stricti iuris*) basis. This meant that the court was supposed to apply a strictly literal reading, rather than considering the intent of the parties. One important consequence of this approach is that liability was all or nothing. Each party simply had or had not fulfilled his or her obligation, and in the latter case was liable for the full value of the agreement. In some respects, a "literal" reading might seem like a good thing. It is a relatively objective standard, which might make it the most fair, and in theory it limits the intervention of the state in what is meant to be a private matter.

Unfortunately, there were problems as well. Such literal reading increased the opportunity for trickery (if not outright fraud), especially in a complicated agreement. Recall that there may well have been an elaborate pair of promises, each referring to actions the other party might or might not take; these could become quite involved. And even if both parties were acting in good faith, something could simply go wrong, which was again especially likely in a complex agreement. Putting conditional penalties on both parties, for instance, could be tricky. If you weren't careful, you could get into a situation in which nothing in the contract was binding until one party made the first move or in which one party's performance was required despite the total failure of the other. And even if the agreement was well thought out, there was a greater chance that such a document could be spoiled by what amounts to a typo [7]. Literal reading could also cause problems if the agreement itself was clear enough, but an unforeseen situation arose in the real world. Suppose someone stipulated to deliver 500 head of cattle, but in fact produced only 499. We might agree that he has not fulfilled his contract, but should he really be in the same position as someone who made the same agreement and then delivered no cattle at all? Toward the end of the

Republic, the law was changed slightly to allow a defendant in a *stipulatio* case to plead that the original agreement had been made under duress or by fraud, but most of the problems remained.

Consensual contracts were all "bilateral." That is, the parties were obligated to each other, though not necessarily in exactly parallel ways. As a result, they were judged on the basis not of "strict law" but of "good faith" (*bonae fidei*). This allowed the trial judge to ignore unnecessary technicalities or trickery, and to recognize partial performance of duties and grant a fraction of the value of the contract in damages. In time, the good faith standard came to be understood to imply certain terms in all agreements of a given type. For instance, it was eventually the case that a seller of goods had to give a warranty of title. That is, if the objects turned out to be someone else's property, then he would have to reimburse the buyer (since the original owner would still be considered the true owner and so could recover the goods in question). This is an advance over the *stipulatio* and its strict-law implications, but consensual contracts had problems of their own.

First, they demanded more of the judge's input than might be desirable (as discussed earlier). Second, being entirely without forms, these contracts were, if anything, harder to prove than *stipulationes*. The same problem actually appears in the law of marriage (Chapter 17); it too was defined primarily by consent (rather than by, say, a license or ceremony), making it difficult to prove whether someone was married. In general, the Roman jurists seemed to have had little interest in purely practical evidentiary problems of this kind. It became normal practice in the case of both kinds of contract to write down the terms of agreement, but until well after our period, this writing did not equal the contract; it was mere evidence (see Chapter 8 on writing). Third, consensual contracts offered the mixed blessing of action at a distance. Since the *stipulatio* required an oral question and answer, the parties had to be in the same place at the same time in order to bring the contract into being. Other contracts, requiring only agreement, could be made by letter, messenger, or any other means. As the Roman world expanded from a city-state, to Italy, to a pan-Mediterranean empire, it became more and more convenient to be able to do business that was not face-to-face. (Even with consensual contracts, business would still have been slowed by human travel times.) But this created problems as well.

In early face-to-face transactions, the deal could have been struck, and price and merchandise exchanged, all more or less at the same time. With contracts made at a distance, these actions could occur at three different times. It was then necessary to account for new issues. What happens if the merchandise is damaged or destroyed between the beginning and end of a sale process? Does either party have a responsibility to see to it that this doesn't happen? What if the parties misunderstand each other as to the terms of a lease? The specific rules that eventually grew up are complicated, and we need not go into the details here. The main point is that these questions, unlike some of the others discussed earlier, do not have an obvious right answer to guide the lawmaker. Say you have paid $5,000 for a horse, and it is struck by lightning before you pick it up from the seller. Whether or not you get your money back, one or the other of you is going to come out the loser, without either necessarily being at fault. Fairness cannot tell the law how to apportion that risk. The Roman solution in general is to put the risk on the buyer, only partially balanced by a requirement that the seller protect the merchandise while it is still in his possession. It has been pointed out that this is at least in line with the fact that the buyer is also the one who stands to lose or gain from fluctuations in, say, the market value of the item once the contract has been made. Parties who wished to divide up the risk differently were generally free to do so by explicit wording in their contracts [8, 14].

Most of the examples just given have been drawn from the law of sale (what the Romans called *emptio venditio*, "buying-selling"), and I want to start from there in the discussion of the specifics of consensual contracts [25]. The basic idea of sale was the exchange of goods for a price, and an agreement that did not fit that model could not be protected by the contract of sale (as in the case of thing-for-thing barter mentioned earlier). The merchandise usually consisted of a physical thing or things, but could also be "non-corporeal," like the right to sue someone or to inherit from someone. It had to be narrowly specified to make the agreement final. You could not technically contract to sell "ten bushels of wheat" (though many negotiations were probably conducted in such terms). A contract came into being only when some particular ten bushels had eventually been measured out. The major seeming exception to the rule is the sale of future produce of some field, but in that case there can be no argument about what is included in the sale, even if one does not immediately know how large or small it will turn out to be. The price also had to be stated (or at least knowable in theory) at the time of agreement. Here there was potentially a real exception to the rule in the case of the sale of future produce. The price could be absolutely fixed (and would be paid even if the crop failed entirely), or one could agree to pay by unit (say, $53 per pound), so that the price would not be known until the crop came in. (In this case, conveniently for the buyer, the price for a failed crop would be $53 x no pounds = $0.) The price was generally up to the parties to negotiate, but in cases of extremely low price, the deal might be construed by the courts as really a gift, merely disguised as a sale. This could matter (a) if the merchandise had not yet been delivered, since the promise of a gift was not enforceable, or (b) if the agreement was between husband and wife, whose gifts to each other were not given legal force.

Other terms that came to be read into contracts of sale include warranty against bad title and against "latent defects" (i.e., defects known to the seller but not revealed or visible on inspection). Standard terms that might be added to a contract of sale included further warranties, redistribution of risk, the location where disputes were to be litigated, schedules of payment or delivery, severability of some individually unenforceable provisions, and conditions of use (say, requiring a new building owner to allow previous tenants to continue occupying, not allowing a slave to be used as a prostitute, or renting a property back to its previous owner).

The contract often today called "hire" (in Latin *locatio conductio*, something like "leasing out/hiring") raises many of the same issues as sale, but has a broader set of applications [5, 6]. The basic idea is the exchange of a price for temporary use of a thing or of someone's labor. Its main use in case of things was to rent out real estate. When it was used for labor, there were two configurations. One could hire persons, normally on a daily basis, for unspecified tasks, or hire out an entire task (say, the building of a house) to someone. These would correspond to contracts for day laborers and general contractors, respectively. The price apparently had to be a fixed amount of money, as in sale [5]. (Here there was another agricultural exception; rents for farm land might be a share of the produce.) The term was fixed by agreement, though the contract could be renewed at will or even tacitly. A person renting some property or contracting for a job had legal responsibilities for the upkeep of the property and the appropriate completion of the work, respectively. The person hiring laborers was, of course, obligated to pay them. The person renting out property was required to do what he could to allow the tenant to have use of it. The nature of this obligation brings out an important point about this contract. The tenant had enforceable rights with respect to the landlord, but not to the property itself. So, for instance, the new owner of a building had no obligations to rental tenants who occupied it. If he evicted them or changed the terms of their leases, they could sue the previous owner/landlord for breach of their contract with him, but that would not get their homes back. Even if that previous owner had sold on the condition that the new owner keep the tenants in their original situation, the latter would not have to restore them if he could afford to absorb the damages from a suit for breach of the contract of sale. And even this might not have much effect, if the previous owner had moved far from the local jurisdiction and thus was able in practice to evade suits from his former tenants. As with sale, additional terms in specific instances might treat timing of payments, periodic approval of work done, timing of delivery, or penalties for failure to meet these terms.

The contract of partnership (Latin *societas*) has a character different from any of the others. It can involve any number of participants. When the agreement is initially made, the partners agree on several things: the purpose of the venture, whether it is a one-time arrangement or ongoing, the shares of the total profits and losses each partner will be responsible for, and the assets that each will commit to the project. These assets might include everything the parties owned, but were usually limited to a fixed amount, occasionally including something intangible like connections. The partnership could involve joint ownership of property (Chapter 14), but this was not necessary, nor did joint ownership necessarily require partnership. The shares of profits and losses did have to be proportional to each other or to the initial contributions. One extreme case – profits without danger of loss – was theoretically possible. Keep in mind, however, that if a proposed partnership were too unfair, the disfavored parties would likely not agree to it in the first place.

If there was no other agreement in place, each partner took an equal share in profits and losses, but the only absolute rule was that no one could be entirely excluded from the profits. The basic legal consequence of the partnership was as follows: if one partner carried out a transaction on behalf of the partnership, the others were liable to him for their shares of the costs (up to the limits of their participation), or, conversely, he was obliged to pay them their shares of the profits. In practice, it is likely that much of this accounting was done on paper, and money changed hands only periodically and/or at the dissolution of the partnership. The method would have been essentially the same as the accounting used, say, by roommates who pay bills and buy food for the household as needed out of their individual pockets, but then periodically equalize their contributions. Note that, as was the case with the contract of hire, rights exist only between persons who have their own contract. A person who sold something "to the partnership" was really selling to the individual partner he was dealing with (unlike the way, for instance, a paper goods supplier today might sell to a small business rather than to the individual owner of that business). If the seller did not get paid because the other partners balked at paying, he had no direct legal recourse against them; he could sue the contracting partner for the full amount.

Another unusual feature of partnership was that, unlike most contracts, it did not necessarily have a natural conclusion. The question then arises of how a partnership might be dissolved. There are several ways. It ended if the initial purpose was achieved. Any partner could renounce the arrangement, and the whole partnership was thereby dissolved and remaining obligations had to be settled. (In principle, this happened immediately, but since the contract operated on a good faith basis, a judge might prevent a partner from taking unfair advantage of the order of payments and expenses.) In fact, if any of the partners wanted to file suit over the operations of the partnership, he or she was automatically considered to have ended the agreement. Finally, if one of the partners died, the partnership was also dissolved, at least in later law. All of this suggests that partnerships were very fragile, and this is true, but it should be noted that the remaining partners (or even the entire original group) could instantly form a "new" partnership if they so desired.

It is worth saying a few words about a very special case of partnership. Many functions of the Roman state (building projects, supply for the army, tax collection) were not carried out by governmental agencies but were instead outsourced to groups of private investors in a bidding process. These groups were called *publicani* (hence the "publicans" of the New Testament). Partnerships formed for this purpose were governed by special rules. They normally survived the death of a partner, whether in diminished form or by replacing that partner with an heir. Some have also suggested that these partnerships had a more corporate identity, rather than existing as a set of purely bilateral obligations as described here, but the evidence is weak.

We have seen one formal contract (*stipulatio*) and three consensual ones (sale, hire, and partnership). Let me introduce two more contracts (one very briefly) to illustrate a third type.

One contract is *pignus*, "pledge" or "mortgage," and it is a so-called real contract [3, 14]. "Real" means that it required not only agreement, but also the actual handing over of a thing (Latin *res*). An item was pledged by a debtor to a creditor to guarantee payment of some obligation. This obligation was perhaps typically from a loan, but could also arise from any other source (e.g., sale, dowry, hire, even a delict). The pledge could be made in advance of the obligation even existing and (if so) could be made conditionally. The creditor could take possession of the pledge, but not sell or (generally) use it unless there was specific agreement on these points. She did not have to return the pledge (or any part of it) until the entire debt was paid. (Roman law also recognized other forms of security, which had somewhat different rules on these points [7, 9].) The same object could be pledged to multiple creditors, though it was best to inform them all of the situation and keep careful track of the total indebtedness to avoid charges of fraud. Similarly, the basic contract for loan of cash (or anything else that would be used up by the borrower) was a "real" contract [8–12]. It was complicated by the fact that it did not include payment of interest, so some additional agreement was typically needed to make the arrangement commercially viable. (There were probably also cases in which the borrower fictionally admitted to having received more from the lender than he actually did. Since he was liable for what he had admitted to, the difference in amounts became the interest.)

We see in this ensemble of contracts some major features of Roman law in general. At a very abstract level, they are designed to protect values external to the law itself. The consensual contracts govern common, important commercial transactions. They bring a predictability to these situations, which encourages economic activity. Moreover, elite Roman culture tended to talk of such commerce as morally difficult. All the more reason, then, to impose certain standards of fair dealing by law. At the same time, the means of achieving those ends tended to follow a logic internal to the law. Old forms of contract were never abolished, even if obsolete, and hence became part of the accumulation. That accumulation may also have encouraged the (already existing) conservatism of the legal community in retaining old categories like formal versus consensual and strict law versus good faith. Hence, the Romans never developed a streamlined theory of contract in general, but kept to their sets of contracts.

13. OWNERSHIP AND POSSESSION

꘎꘎꘎꘎꘎꘎꘎꘎꘎

THIS IS A particularly technical area of the law, and the extent of my simplification will be greater than usual. "Ownership" is, in general, the right (or a set of rights) to control a thing, a piece of property. While there are differences between Roman and common law in this area, it would be fair to say that the Romans had a notion of ownership, which they called *dominium*. (I will also sometimes use the alternative English term "title" as a synonym.) Since ownership is a matter of rights, the question of who "owns" something is necessarily a question about legal rules. Both Roman and common law also give some recognition to the notion of "possession." At least initially, the question of who "possesses" something is a matter of fact, not of law, but over time both systems turn possession into something that is more like a lesser degree of ownership. The kind of "things" that can be owned in Roman law are quite varied, including movable property (money, tools), real estate (both land and buildings), living beings (livestock, pets, human slaves), and more abstract rights (the right to collect a debt, to extract clay from a piece of land, to file certain kinds of lawsuit). The first two sections of this chapter will treat the basic rules of ownership and possession, respectively. The third section will then discuss how the two notions were brought closer together over time. The next chapter will discuss some kinds of rights over property that are less expansive than ownership and possession.

OWNERSHIP

Ownership is, as we just noted, a set of rights over a piece of property. In Roman law, the owner of something has nearly absolute and exclusive rights over it. Later in this chapter (and especially in the next), we will see some of the complications hiding in the word "nearly," but to start, let us say that the owner has total authority to use, destroy, or "alienate" (i.e., sell or give away) his property. Following on this definition, the most important questions about ownership, then, are how does one become an owner in theory, and how does one prove it in practice?

If something does not already have an owner, you can generally just claim it as your own. There are, of course, complications, but the situation doesn't actually arise often (catching wild animals would probably be the most common instance), so we can just leave this first approximation alone. Somewhat more important is the rule that additions to an already-owned object belong to the original owner. So, for instance, you get to keep the fruit from your trees, the offspring of your livestock, and even land that builds up along any riverbank property you own. Manufacturing presented a somewhat trickier case, but the general idea seems to have been that an object created from raw materials was a new thing and (at least initially) belonged to the person who created it. These ways of gaining ownership apply only once to a given object, but that same object can then change hands any number of times, so the really important rules are about just how this transfer is allowed to happen. There are several "modes" of transferring property directly from one person to another. It would not be worthwhile to go into all the details here, but one complication will be unavoidable. Two of these modes required a certain amount of formality or ritual to carry them out, and one had other prerequisites (both parties present at the same time and place; both citizens). So why not just stick with the simplest mode? Roman law divided property into two categories for which there are no precise modern equivalents: *res mancipi* (primarily Italian land, slaves, and certain livestock) and *res nec mancipi* (pretty much everything else, including, most notably, cash). Ownership of *res mancipi* could technically be transferred only by the more complex modes of transfer, even if both parties would have preferred to skip them. That is, the mere fact that the owner of some *res mancipi* gave or sold it to you did *not* make you the owner unless you used the proper formalities. (In this respect, it was like the checking of title required for the sale of certain big-ticket items like real estate or cars, but not needed to buy a hamburger or a bicycle.) That didn't mean the seller could keep it; the contract he agreed to required him to hand it over. But if another person then got her hands on it, you were in trouble. You still weren't the owner, and you didn't have a contract with *her*. There was, however, a way to avoid parts of this mess, especially when the different parties cooperated with each other. This was called *usucapio*. If you acquired an item in good faith (say, by buying it) and then retained it for an appropriate amount of time (one or two years, depending on what it was), the system would act as if the rituals had been carried out in the first place.

The rights of ownership were protected by a procedure called *vindicatio*: the parties both stated their claims to the same object, and the judge decided whose case was better. Much of the time this would have been a reasonably easy question to decide, at least as a matter of law. But looking at the rules for acquisition just described, we can see the potential for trouble. In principle, to show ownership you would need to prove that you had acquired an object by an appropriate means from someone else who had gotten it correctly, who had also gotten it properly, and so on, back to the original acquisition. Aside from the fact that this chain could be extremely long, each individual step might be hard to prove. (Romans also didn't have private firms like modern "title companies" that tried to keep track of the ownership of real estate.) The rituals required for validity did not leave automatic traces of themselves, and they might well have been omitted by previous parties who didn't need to worry about legalities. Say, for instance, you buy a car from a man who had gotten it as a hand-me-down from his older sister. *Usucapio* could help by making some of the individual steps easier to prove (time lapse might be easier to show than ritual), but it also created problems of its own. While valuable in the long term, *usucapio* left a short-term problem. If, for instance, you bought some item of *res mancipi* without ceremony (presumably assuming you would eventually "usucapt" it, i.e., gain ownership by *usucapio*), there would be a period after the sale when you were not technically the owner (and so could not enforce your rights by the procedure just described), but when the technical owner (the seller) would have no reason (and perhaps no right) to enforce your would-be ownership against a third party. The problems were never entirely resolved during our period, but some changes in the law chipped away at them (whether or not that was the original intention). The next two sections of this chapter will discuss those changes.

POSSESSION

As we have just seen, the rules of ownership had a certain logic, but were in danger of getting too far removed from reality. Anyone who could win ownership in court probably deserved it, but many people who were equally deserving likely could not prove ownership. Eventually, the Edict was used to create a more flexible, more realistic situation. The general idea was to give some legal protection to the mere possession of property (when ownership had not been established), and the means of doing so was not the *vindicatio*, but rather an order from the praetor called an interdict. Protecting ownership is an attractive idea for a couple of reasons. First, it can be a partial stand-in for ownership. That is, all other things being equal, the original possessor of an item is more likely to be the true owner than a later one, and the order of possession is likely to be a lot easier to prove. Second, even if possession does not always line up with ownership, protecting the former can help limit antisocial behavior. You don't, for instance, want people using force to recover anything to which they believe they have title (no matter how sincere that belief), since either party, or even innocent bystanders, could be permanently harmed. Protecting possession encourages the resolution of property disputes through proper legal procedure.

An interdict was essentially a conditional order. For instance:

> With whichever person the slave at issue in this case lived for the greater part of the past year (as long as he was not there by stealth, force, or permission), I forbid force to be used to prevent that person from taking him back [the so-called interdict *utrubi*, named after its first word in Latin].

or

> From which place you (or your slaves or your manager) ejected that man (or his slaves or his manager) by force within the year, although he was in possession (as long as that was not by force, stealth, or permission), you must restore him to that place [the interdict *unde vi*].

These are "conditional" because they are so general. Note that the wording does not specify any particular slave or land; it uses generic phrases like "whichever." As a result, the praetor could issue it more or less on request, since it automatically gave the targeted party an out. If the target was confident that his possession was legal, he could simply ignore the order. He was not in any danger until and unless the first petitioner initiated a suit for the (supposed) violation of the order, and even then the defendant could argue that the order didn't apply because the condition had not been met.

In a *vindicatio*, both parties were trying to prove the same thing (ownership). It was quite likely that neither could do so decisively, and it was possible that neither was in fact the owner. The wording of the various edicts was designed to limit trials to a consideration of the relationship between the two parties. Who, for instance, had been in possession first? Did one use force against the other? This makes it much more likely that the trial court will produce the technically correct result. On the other hand, this correct result will not reliably be the right one in the broader sense. That is, you might well lose a suit over possession even if you are truly the owner. This is particularly true in a situation in which more than two parties are involved. Say you are in a dispute with a neighbor over a piece of property. If he transfers it to a friend, that person hasn't taken any prohibited action against you, and so you will not generally be able to reclaim possession from her. Now, even if some of these problems arise in using the interdicts, all is not necessarily lost. The option of *vindicatio* is still open if you can prove ownership, and at this point the general nature of its claim ("I am the owner") becomes an advantage.

THE *ACTIO PUBLICIANA*

Another procedure was introduced in the mid first century BC to try to reduce the importance of formalities in property transfer. This was called the *actio Publiciana*. It was a modified version of the *vindicatio* procedure, but it operated with the fiction that the would-be owner had held on to the object long enough for *usucapio* to take place. This entirely eliminated the short-term problem of the buyer-who-was-not-yet-owner. Now, this was not a perfect solution, since the time lapse built into the idea of *usucapio* was not entirely pointless in origin. It made problems easier to fix when something went substantively wrong in a transaction. Say, for instance, I sell you a disputed parcel of land, but the person with a competing claim does not realize this until after the original sale. Thus the introduction of the *actio Publiciana* gained greater efficiency at the cost of making bad transactions slightly more likely.

14. OTHER RIGHTS
OVER PROPERTY

✧✧✧✧✧✧✧✧

O WNERSHIP AND POSSESSION are both standardized sets or packages of rights over pieces of property, but Roman law also allowed the packages to be broken up in other ways. The owner could retain his title to an item but transfer control over it (for a time), or retain both title and control while granting specific rights (say, the right to walk across his land). This greater flexibility was of commercial value, since it gave owners a variety of ways to exploit their property and allowed them to deal with a variety of other business partners. But, as we will see, these partial rights were also useful for other reasons. The first section of this chapter treats temporary but near-total transfers of rights (*usus* and *usufructus*); the second treats a set of more limited rights (called "servitudes") that could be traded. The third section treats rights a neighbor could claim over next-door property. The last one will cover the limitations produced by joint ownership.

USUS AND USUFRUCT

These are the rights to the use of an object with (usufruct) or without (*usus*) the right to keep the "fruits" of the property (e.g., fruit from an orchard or ore from a mine, rental income, offspring of livestock). The combination package, usufruct, is more common, and, since the rules for this and for *usus* by itself are largely the same, I will speak only of usufruct in what follows. In principle, there could be a usufruct of anything (originally only a thing not meant to be consumed — say, livestock or tools, but not cash or grain), but in practice it was usually used for real estate. Usufruct could be created by the various rituals used to transfer ownership in general (in fact, the right of usufruct is treated as a type of property in its own right). In this way one could give or sell usufruct in a commercial transaction. However, this is not actually how it was normally used. The ordinary way to create a usufruct was by will; ownership of an item was left to one person, and usufruct of it to another. So, for instance, a man might pass title of the family house to his children, but leave the use of it to his wife. In fact, provision for widows seems to give rise to more usufructs than all other scenarios combined, and may have been the origin of the entire concept. It could also be used in the division of an estate among heirs who wanted to retain some parts more or less in common.

The fact that usufruct is so closely tied to this one social situation makes sense of a number of the specific rules that govern it. For instance, a usufruct could not be created to last longer than the lifetime of the person who was to benefit. Contrast that to modern copyright, which substantially outlives the actual author. This is because the value of copyright lies primarily in its sale, so the longer term helps the buyer and (because she can get a better price) the author. Usufruct is not thought of (primarily) in such commercial terms, so it does not need to run longer; it runs long enough to help a spouse left behind. (A term *shorter* than life could be fixed at the time it was created, though this seems to have been rare.) Technically, usufructs could not be resold – again, we see its noncommercial origins – but there was a significant loophole. The holder of the usufruct could rent or sell the "enjoyment" of it. This made exploitation of the property easier, since you could take simple, fixed cash payment rather than having to run the old family farm yourself. Still, the technical holder of the usufruct remained a middleman between the owner and the end user.

Moreover, he was a middleman in an important practical sense as well. The holder of any usufruct, whether rented out or not, had responsibilities to the owner. He couldn't damage the property. If there was loss to the property – say, a window was blown out in a storm or animals in a flock died naturally over the course of a year – he had to make it good, whether out of the profits or out of his own resources. (The holder of the usufruct was held to the standard of how a "good *pater familias*" would care for his own property.) This provision is not surprising, and similar terms exist in other relationships in which one person has temporary custody of another's property. In this case, however, there is a tighter and more specific restriction. The holder of a usufruct was not allowed to make changes that would alter the fundamental character of the property, even if these changes were arguably improvements – for example, replacing a small building with a larger one, replacing shade trees with fruit trees, mining on crop land, plastering bare walls, or even installing gutters. Note that this restriction is not technically negotiable; it is built into the definition of usufruct (though, of course, an owner who really did not care what the holder of usufruct was doing to her property could simply choose not to take legal action to stop it.) Again, this limits the flexibility and thus the commercial value of usufruct, but makes reasonable sense if (as just suggested) usufruct is meant as temporary support for one person until the "real" owner takes over. Note also that if the nature of the property was dramatically altered by *outside* forces (say, if a house burned entirely to the ground), the usufruct came to an end.

SERVITUDES

Usufruct gives its holder broad enough rights that we can think of it as near to ownership, but with a few defined limitations. Servitudes, on the other hand, are very specific rights over a piece of property that in most respects remains under the control of the actual owner. Servitudes are "real" rights in the technical sense of being attached to things (Latin *res*), not to people (compare the "real" contracts discussed in Chapter 12 or the English term "real estate"). More specifically, they were always built into a pair of adjacent pieces of real estate. When a servitude exists in one of these pairs, the person who happens to own one property (the "dominant" one) at any given time always has that right over the person who happens to own the other ("servient") one at that time. Suppose you own a farm with the servitude right to draw water from the spring on my (next-door) farm. Then, suppose that we sell the farms to our respective sisters. Your sister then automatically acquires the right to get her water from my sister's farm (while neither you nor I keep any rights). There are a great many specific servitudes – for example, passage over another's property, drawing water, allowing/preventing dripping or smoke from another's building, blocking/allowing light. At least some details could be set individually (say, the time or mode in which the rights could be used), and it is possible that entirely new servitudes could be created as long as they fit the general rules [24].

Servitudes were usually created by agreement between the two owners, though the agreement had to be validated by appropriate ritual. This commonly took place at the time of a sale (with the old owner retaining certain rights over a part of the property he was selling). It might also commonly be done at times when a formerly unitary property was divided, such as when joint heirs wished to separate their shares of that property. Another way to gain a servitude was simply to assert and use the right for a sufficiently long time. This was an unusual method of acquiring rights in Roman law, but it is paralleled in common law by the law of so-called easements. This possibility existed in earlier and later periods (with some technical differences) but not for some period in between, perhaps roughly the first two centuries BC. When it did exist, a property owner might specify that use was with his permission (which he could revoke), and that would block formation of the servitude [23f, i].

Unlike usufruct, servitudes could in principle last forever, and in theory it was not possible to create one with a built-in time limit. The owner of a dominant property could renounce it by appropriate ritual, and that would eliminate the relationship between the two properties from that point forward. The servitude would also automatically disappear if both properties came to be owned by the same person (you can't have a right against yourself), even if they were later divided again. Most distinctive to servitude is loss by disuse, the flip side of acquisition by assertion. There were two versions of this process. So-called positive servitudes involved the right to use the other person's property directly (e.g., passage, drawing water). These were lost by simple nonuse for a specified length of time (a year or two). Written notices might serve to reinforce the existence of such rights [23a, c, m]. "Negative" servitudes, on the other hand, involved the right to stop the other person from certain uses of their property (e.g., discharging smoke, blocking light). These counted as "unused" only as long as that other person was actually taking potentially forbidden action (e.g., has actually built a house that blocks your light). Since asserting and denying rights was important to keeping them, it was common to post notices asserting your rights (or denying others'), and many of these have survived, inscribed on stone (see [24]). This general idea of loss by disuse is also paralleled in the modern law of easement. (Some universities where I have worked have similar notices written on metal plaques embedded in the sidewalks around the edges of the campus. On these, the university regents assert that passage is by permission only and so does not create an easement.)

In addition to the rules of creation and loss of servitudes, and the lists of specific types, there were a few general principles about how all of them could be exercised. Most of these show that the servitude rights were not just technically attached to the physical properties, but were thought of as closely tied to them. First, the servitude holder could not demand any help from the other property owner. You might have a right to walk across your neighbor's land or draw water from his spring, but he didn't have to clear a path or provide containers. Second, you had to minimize the disruption caused by exercising your rights. Driving a herd across your neighbor's land to get to market was no excuse for wandering through the farmhouse, much less grazing on his crops. Finally, the benefit from your exploitation of your right had to be tied to the land it came with. For instance, you could draw water to irrigate your farm, but not to sell or even to share with your neighbor on the other side. So servitudes were narrower than, say, the mineral rights often sold in the American West, which are specifically designed for commercial exploitation.

DAMNUM INFECTUM

Though they are not conventionally classed with usufruct and servitudes, there are other legal institutions that can be usefully discussed in the same context. We've already noted the existence of several servitudes that prevented one neighbor from building on his own land in various ways that could interfere with another neighbor's enjoyment of her property. There was also a more general mechanism to prevent a neighbor from using a property in a way that would damage yours; this is called *damnum infectum* ("damage not yet done"). If you feared such damage, you could go to the praetor who had the power to order the neighbor to provide security (in the form of a binding promise to pay restitution) against that possibility. This procedure could be used in the course of construction or mere neglect that threatened neighboring property.

JOINT OWNERSHIP

In Roman law, as in the United States and England today, it is possible for something to have more than one owner at once. This would be most common in the case of the heirs to a given estate (the children typically inheriting the family farm jointly) or business partners owning the assets of the business together. (Note that there is a difference between two partners who *each* own a store and two partners *both* of whom own half of two stores. The law allows either.) In theory, any number of people could own the same object. Moreover, while equal shares were common, any division of percentages could be used. In many respects, each owner could exercise the full rights of ownership as if she had no co-owners. She could reclaim the object from nonowners and was free to sell her share of ownership (to the extent allowed by the law of sale in general). The main problems were encountered, of course, in conflicts between owners. In theory, any owner could veto any use of the property intended by another, though there was no right to "roll back" actions already taken. Joint owners were also liable to the other owners if they were responsible for damage to the property. Contrast the sole owner of, say, a house, who was broadly free even to burn it down. It was also possible for any of the joint owners to go to court to force a division of property, with the result that each person would be the sole owner of some part, instead of each owning a share of the whole. This required accounting for the relative shares of the parties, their respective wishes, and the preservation of overall value (no one benefits, after all, from dividing a chariot by sawing it in half). It is important to note in the case of business partnerships that Roman law had no corporations, so you couldn't share ownership of "the business" as a whole, only of specific assets: buildings, equipment, items of stock, (slave) employees, and so on. More abstract aspects of the business (e.g., debts) could be shared indirectly by way of the contract of partnership (see Chapter 12), and liability could be partially limited by the original contributions to the partnership. Still, there was no way to automatically link ownership to partnership.

15. INHERITANCE

❖❖❖❖❖❖❖❖

A NY SOCIETY WITH private property needs rules to determine how to distribute a person's things when he dies. In Rome, this need was particularly acute because inheritance was more important than it is today as a means of acquiring wealth. Business opportunities certainly existed, but they were relatively rare and risky. Fewer people "made" fortunes, and more were born into them. In principle, a Roman citizen was able to distribute his property to other Roman citizens after death in virtually any way he desired. This was done by leaving a document we call a "will" (and the Romans called a *testamentum*). Over time, certain limitations arose, some of which were then weakened or even rescinded. The writer of a will named one or more heirs to the whole estate (in potentially unequal shares), but also had the option of first giving specific items or amounts off the top as "legacies." If someone failed to write a will, or if the will were judged invalid for failing to meet one of its many formal requirements, then the estate was distributed by a standardized set of rules. The general principle at all times was to give equal shares to the closest relatives, though the definition of "closest relative" shifted somewhat over time. At the same time, a device evolved that allowed some restrictions to be evaded (by instructing a beneficiary to pass on wealth).

The first section will explain the two ways in which a Roman will could distribute the deceased's property; as we will see, there were rules about both the substance and the form of the will. The following section will consider what happened when someone died without leaving a will.

WILLS

The formal requirements of the will were that it be written, that it be in Latin (a rule eventually relaxed), that it be witnessed by seven other Roman citizens, and that it name the heir(s) by means of established legal formulas. Also, if the direct descendants were not to be made heirs, they had to be explicitly disinherited.

Every Roman will had to name one or more "heirs." In the simplest case, the heir took on everything the deceased had to her name: property, cash, debts, obligations. If there were more than one heir, then every one of them became a joint owner of the property (and joint debtor). The shares could be in any proportion spelled out in the will (say, one person inheriting two-thirds of the estate with two other persons getting one-sixth each), but equal division was perhaps the most common ([3] shows a much more elaborate division). In case one or more of the would-be heirs did not accept the inheritance (for instance, if the assets did not cover the debts, or if the heir had died already and the will had not been edited), substitute heirs could also be named [18].

Once at least one heir was named, the writer of the will could stop, but there were additional options available. Before the principal division among the heirs, specific gifts could be given to named individuals [18, 19]. These gifts are called "legacies," and the persons who received them are called "legatees." Originally, there were no limitations on these legacies, but over time they came to be abused (or at least so it was thought). That is, some wills gave away so much in legacies that the heirs were left with nothing but debts. Different solutions were tried, but the one that was ultimately enacted (by a *lex Falcidia* of 40 BC) was a rule that at least one-fourth of the estate had to be reserved for the heirs.

With some small partial exceptions to be addressed later, the writer of the will had great freedom to choose his beneficiaries. On the one hand, no one had an absolute claim to the inheritance. In particular, it should be noted that the eldest child had no special rights, as they do in some systems. Nor did male children have any advantage over their sisters. Nor did spouses have any particular rights. On the other hand, there were only a few classes of persons excluded from inheriting. Beneficiaries had to be Roman citizens. A beneficiary had to be a "specified person" at the time of the writing of the will: no corporate entities (though some, such as cities, were eventually permitted to be beneficiaries; see [19]) and no persons not yet conceived. Most importantly, the writer could specify only his own immediate heirs. He could not dictate where the property would go when they in turn died.

A will might be challenged in court after the writer's death. This could be done on formal or substantive grounds. An informal convention arose that at least one-quarter of the estate should go to the immediate descendants of the deceased unless there were some specific reason otherwise. If they did not get their share and the will did not offer an (adequate) justification, they could challenge the "undutiful" will in court. In such cases, the persons trying to break the will were arguing directly for their own interests. Those who argued that a will was invalid on technical grounds (say, failure to use the standard formulas or the legal incompetence of the deceased) presumably had similar interests, but thought that they would be more likely to succeed by an indirect approach. The courts did not attempt to "fix" defective wills; they only decided whether the will was (entirely) valid or (entirely) invalid.

Other restrictions were also put in place from time to time that had little to do with the goals of inheritance law as such. The law punished certain people (e.g., convicted criminals) and discouraged certain kinds of behavior (e.g., childlessness, beginning from the time of the emperor Augustus) by restricting the ability to receive inheritances. This kind of rule might be compared to the use of tax policy today as a way to encourage or discourage certain actions without requiring or forbidding them outright (say, buying a house or dipping into retirement savings, respectively). So couples that were childless or of too-diverse statuses had limited (and sometimes no) ability to inherit from each other. Perhaps more important was a law of the mid second century BC that forbade women to be made heirs in the wills of wealthy persons (though they could still collect under the rules of intestate inheritance; see the following section). The law seems to have gone out of force by the beginning of the empire.

INTESTATE SUCCESSION

"Intestate succession" is the distribution of property when someone dies without a usable will. "Intestate" means "without a will"; "succession" refers to the passing down of the property. This situation arises when someone dies without leaving behind a will or if the will is invalid for some reason. So the persons who challenged a will in court were normally the persons who would benefit under the rules of intestate succession. If the will were to be ruled invalid for any reason, they could then collect automatically.

The precise rules for intestate succession changed somewhat over time (and I will discuss some of those changes later), but the general shape of the system remained the same. The general idea was that, if there was no will, the property would go to the nearest relative, who would become an "heir" in the sense just discussed [20]. If there was more than one equally close relative (say, three children of a deceased father), then they became joint heirs in equal shares. As part of the definition of what counted as a "close" relative, the law divided the potential beneficiaries into a few categories (the details varied over time). If there was no one in the first category, or if all the people in the first category refused the inheritance, then those in the second category would have a chance, and so on. Within each category it was sometimes important to measure "degree" of relationship. This was just a matter of counting how many links there were between two people on the family tree. So, for instance, siblings are two degrees apart from each other (one link up, one back down), while first cousins are four degrees apart. It will be easier to see how this works by looking at the rules in a little more detail, and that will require talking about the historical development and about two important points of Roman family law. As for historical development, we can say for our purposes there were three sets of rules over time: the statutory rules, the praetorian rules, and the imperial ones, in that order.

The main point of family law to note here is that for inheritance purposes, children are descended from their father, but not (at least originally) from their mother. (See Chapter 17 for a broader perspective on family law, and in particular the difficulties defining "family.") Note that this is not a matter of discrimination against women as such; it means that (at least originally) a woman's "real" family was the one she was born into, not the one created by her marriage. This same structure is reflected in the existence of a category of relatives called "agnates," a word that exists in English only to translate the Latin *agnatus*. These are persons who are both descended from the same male ancestor and through men only. (The intermediate steps have to be male, but the two ends do *not*. On average, as many of your agnates will be women as men.) The "agnatic" family, defined by ties of this sort, may be contrasted with the "nuclear" family of husband, wife, and children. The second point of family law is that the former owner of an ex-slave counted as a relative for many inheritance purposes, but in what follows I will assume that everyone was born a free person.

The statutory rules were part of the Twelve Tables, and so date back at least to 450 BC. They divided potential heirs into only three categories: (1) *Sui Heredes*: These are the immediate descendants of the deceased, normally his children, but potentially his sons' children if they survived their father(s). Boys and girls inherited equally and regardless of birth order. Children who had been given their independence before their father's death were not included. For the reason just given, women by definition did not have *sui heredes*, so in this case one would have to jump to the second category. (2) *Proximus Agnatus*: This is a little trickier than it might look at first. On the one hand, the category isn't just "agnate," but "nearest agnate": if the nearest one doesn't accept, the "next agnate" has no claim. Instead you jump to the third category. On the other hand, there can be more than one "nearest," if several people have the same relationship. Say I die leaving behind no children, but several siblings. My brothers and sisters (two degrees removed) are equally my nearest agnates. My father's brothers and sisters (three degrees away from me) get a shot only if I left *no* siblings of my own in the first place. (3) *Gentiles*: members of the same clan (*gens*). The nature of Roman clans is somewhat unclear, and their role in inheritance remains almost entirely mysterious. All we really know about this class is that it was specified in the rule. The most striking feature of this list from a modern point of view is the absence of spouses: under this system, husbands and wives do not inherit from each other without a will. In that context, however, it is worth reiterating that these are only the rules for what happened without a will. Nothing prevents or even discourages a husband or wife from choosing to leave everything to the other.

Although the rules of intestate succession were clearly treated in statute law, this was one of the areas in which the Edict effectively changed the rules. The precise dates are unclear, but by the first century BC the classes just listed had been replaced by a somewhat similar but longer list: (1) *Liberi*: same as *sui heredes*, already described, but emancipated children are included. (2) *Legitimi*: a mixed group including a father who had freed his children and the "nearest agnate" as defined earlier. (3) *Cognati*: These are any blood relatives, whether or not they are agnates. Here one does work outward through up to seven degrees of relationship until one or more heirs can be found. (4) Spouses: Only if there are no (willing) *cognati* do spouses inherit from a spouse who does not leave a will. (Interestingly, gifts from live spouses were illegal altogether; see Chapter 16.) The general tendency of these changes was to give greater force to the ties of the biological family (as opposed to structures brought about by legal processes) and, to a lesser extent, to give the nuclear family some respect, though still less than that of the "agnatic" view of the family.

The third phase does not involve a systematic updating like the Edict's revisions of the statutory rules. Rather, there were a couple of imperial enactments of around the same time (mid second century AD), and with a shared underlying motivation. Under the *SC Tertullianum*, a mother inherits her children's estate as if she were a sister, which puts her ahead of half-siblings, more distant *cognati*, and (in the case of an illegitimate child) all relatives except a son's child. However, this was thought of as a special privilege for the mother and was available only if she had done her civic "duty" by giving birth to three or more children. Under the *SC Orphitianum*, a mother's children are *legitimi* with respect to her (and thus get first chance, since she has no *liberi*). Both of these decrees act to make mothers and their biological children close relatives for inheritance purposes. The combined effect was a major victory for the nuclear family over the agnatic.

Children born outside of wedlock had no legal ties to their biological fathers. Their basic status – free or slave; citizenship – came from their mothers', but as noted earlier, inheritance doesn't work the same way. Thus, under the first two schemes, the illegitimate children of a Roman woman had no rights of intestate inheritance. A late (mid second century AD?) reinterpretation of the notion of *cognati* recognized them as blood relatives to their mothers and so potentially in line to inherit. Still, this left them behind all their mothers' agnates. It was only with the *SC Orphitianum* that they clearly inherited from their mothers (though still never from their natural fathers).

FIDEICOMMISSA

While the Roman will was already very flexible in itself, a device eventually arose to allow it to do even more. This is called the *fideicommissum* – "entrusting" something to the "faith" of the heir. It involved leaving property to an heir along with instructions to pass some or all of it to other persons. This device had at least three different uses. It could be used to evade the various restrictions on who could benefit from a will, such as noncitizens, corporate entities (say, your hometown), or (under later law) the childless. It could be used to extend the owner's control over his property beyond the immediate distribution to the heirs. For instance, he might leave his property to his wife, with the specification that she then leave it back to their child when she dies. In principle, this method could have been used to create permanent control of the property, but in practice the Roman courts did not allow a will to reach further than persons who could be specifically identified at the time of death (roughly, persons living at the time of the will and their children). Finally, and somewhat surprisingly, it could be used to create what amounts to a partial or informal will. Eventually, it became permissible to leave a stand-alone *fideicommissum* without a will and have it enforced by the courts. In this case, the estate would technically go to heirs determined by the rules of intestate inheritance, but they would then carry out the *fideicommissum* by passing on some or all of that property.

Initially, the *fideicommissum* was an act of faith. The heir(s) had no legal obligation to carry out its instructions. That changed around the turn of the millennium under the emperor Augustus, who gave certain magistrates the authority to enforce these provisions. After this big change, a series of decrees over the first and second centuries trimmed the power of the *fideicommissum* back a little. In particular, the use of the device to leave property to people not otherwise entitled to receive it was eliminated. Note, however, that this still left the possibility of using the *fideicommissum* to extend control over time or for a partial/informal will. Another use was to establish income-producing funds for some ongoing purpose [18, 20]. In particular, they might be used for remembrances of the deceased and/or for upkeep of her tomb or for charity (which might indirectly contribute to remembrance).

16. WOMEN AND PROPERTY

꧁꧂꧁꧂꧁꧂꧁꧂꧁

A S IN MOST (probably all) ancient societies, women had no part in public law. They could not vote or hold public office. For essentially the same reason (if less obviously so), they could not serve as witnesses to formal legal acts or represent others in court. In private law, however, they had surprisingly broad rights. In fact, it has been noted that women were in many respects freer under Roman law than under some "modern" European systems of only a couple of centuries ago. At any rate, it is generally fair to say that the private law presumed that men and women were to be treated in the same way, unless specific exception was made in some specific circumstance. Women could own property, be held liable for crimes, make contracts, and go to court to sue and be sued. They could inherit property, which (as we noted in the previous chapter) was of great financial importance. This chapter will treat the circumstances in which women were treated differently. It will also mention a few areas of the law that have particular effect on women, but that in the end are driven more by the idea of "family" than by any views of gender. (Note also that a woman with a living father had no property rights, just as her brothers did not [see the previous chapter]. In this chapter, I will be speaking of women who are not in power unless explicitly specified.)

WOMEN AND MARRIAGE

Marriage in itself had nearly no effect on a woman's legal status. If she had been under her father's authority, she remained there. If she had been *sui iuris*, she remained so, and her husband gained no claim over her property. Neither spouse had an obligation to support the other. The situation I have just described was the normal one, but there was a potential major exception. The parties could choose a form of marriage (typically, but not necessarily, at the time it was contracted) that would result not just in their being married, but in the woman passing into the *manus* (literally "hand") of her new husband. In this case, if her father was alive, her husband essentially took his place. If she had been *sui iuris*, she returned to essentially the position of a daughter to her husband. Only he could own property. Anything that did come to her became his. He had personal authority over her, though it seems not to have extended to the right of life and death, even in theory. If her husband died intestate, she could inherit from him as one of his *sui heredes* (contrast the normal position of wives as described in Chapter 15). *Manus* seems to have been an early feature of the law, but there is no clear evidence that it was ever a standard part of marriage. Whatever the early situation, by the late Republic it seems to have become (if it wasn't already) extremely rare.

The one noteworthy constraint that marriage placed on a woman's property applied to her husband's as well. Gifts between spouses were not legally valid. Within the marriage this rule was probably not particularly important. If, say, a husband provided his wife with a piece of jewelry or even a house of her own, it would not matter much whether ownership actually changed hands. But if a third party then became involved, the technicalities would become important. The wife could not pawn the jewelry or rent out the house, since she was not the owner, and no one would want to do business if she could not give assurances. (Again, this works both ways. The husband couldn't pawn the watch his wife gave him.) Moreover, if the marriage broke up, there would have to be an accounting. The normal procedure seems to have been to allow each spouse to keep any specific gifts in the settlement, so long as they made up their value out of their own pocket. Some persons apparently tried to evade the rule, by, say, having one spouse pay a debt for another or give a gift to an in-law, but the law rejected these attempts when they were detected.

GUARDIANSHIP OF WOMEN

More significant to a woman's property rights than marriage was the presence of a so-called guardian (*tutor*). The word is the same one used to describe the administrator who took care of the property of a minor child, but the guardian of an adult woman had a much smaller role. Guardians of either sort came into being in the same ways. A father in his will might specify guardians for all his minor children and for his adult daughters. If he did not do so, the "nearest agnate" might be appointed (Chapter 15; for women this ceased to be an option in the mid first century AD). If this were not possible, then the state could appoint a guardian [17]. (Note that the husband, if any, has no place in any of this.) One thing that made the case of adult women different from that of children is that it was possible (and apparently common) to leave the woman her own choice of guardians. This became particularly important when the courts decided that the right was ongoing, that is, that she could replace her tutor at will.

Wherever he had come from, the guardian of an adult woman had a fairly limited function. Unlike the guardian of children, he could not himself undertake any transactions with her property. He could only veto her decisions [12]. Moreover, he could act only in certain cases. Roughly, he could prevent the alienation (sale or gift) of so-called *res mancipi* (Chapter 13), the acceptance of an inheritance, and the making of a will on her part. So, for instance, he could block (but not force) the sale of slaves or land, but he had no say at all in her using cash to purchase something. Also unlike the guardian of children, the adult woman's guardian had no responsibility to her, and so could not be sued or forced to give security. In at least one area, he was allowed to have what we might see as a conflict of interest. If a man became tutor as nearest agnate and exercised his power to prevent the woman from making a will, then he would eventually inherit from her because she would die intestate, and by definition he was at the top of the eligibility list for her estate. From the Roman point of view this seems to have been a desirable outcome because it kept property "in the family."

Over time, there was a trend toward reducing what authority the guardian did have. First, it was not uncommon for a woman to have a guardian over whom she had some other form of leverage, say, a freedman who owed her deference. Second, the ability to choose a tutor, and especially to do so repeatedly, meant that uncooperative guardians could be removed. Short of this, magistrates could step in on an "emergency" basis if a woman's guardian was unavailable. This seems to have become routine, even in cases in which the tutor was simply unwilling rather than unable.

DOWRY

Husbands and wives theoretically did not give gifts within the marriage, but it was conventional to begin the relationship with a substantial transfer from the wife (or her family or friends) to the husband. This seems to have been a larger gift than we would expect of a "wedding present" but typically less than the bride's eventual full inheritance. While the law did not require dowry at all, there were many rules about how it was to be treated when it was given. A dowry could be composed of any kind of property, ranging from cash and real estate (the most common) to personal items (say, clothes and jewelry) to incorporeals (like the right to collect a debt or relief from a servitude). The formal ownership of the property was a matter of some dispute and may have changed over time, but in practice it was treated as the husband's for the duration of the marriage. Certainly, he was entitled to any "fruits" of the property. If the marriage did end, however, the dowry typically reverted to the woman.

The earliest rules for dowry are unclear, in part because of the usual evidentiary problems regarding early times, in part because divorce during this period is not well understood. The classical rules (in this case from around the second century BC) for the recovery of dowry depend on knowing its source. Roughly, dowry that came from the bride's father was called *profecticia*; coming from anyone else (including herself) it was called *adventicia*. If the husband died before the wife, she (or her father, if still alive) could reclaim either. If she died first, her father could reclaim *profecticia*, less one-fifth per child she left behind; the husband kept *adventicia* unless some other plan had been specified by the giver at the time it was given. The situation in a divorce was more complicated. If the wife initiated the divorce (or could be shown to be at fault), the husband could recover various fractions of the dowry based on the number of children and as a penalty for the wife's misbehavior. If the husband initiated the divorce (or was at fault), the wife kept the whole dowry, regardless of the number of children. (He was not required to pay a penalty for misbehavior, but his repayment of the dowry might be put on an accelerated schedule.) "Fault" is not well defined by our sources, but seems to center on moral and especially on sexual impropriety. Note that any extramarital sex by the wife was adultery, permitting (and later requiring) her husband to divorce her. The husband committed an offense only by having sex with "respectable" women; the next-door neighbor was forbidden, but the (slave) maid or a prostitute was acceptable.

The rules just stated were the standards assumed by the law, but most of them could be adjusted by the mutual agreement of the parties at the time the marriage was contracted.

17. FAMILY LAW

❧❧❧❧❧❧❧❧❧

THE FAMILY SEEMS to be an important institution within all societies. So it is not surprising that societies, modern or Roman, with sophisticated legal systems have elaborate rules about those families. They regulate, for instance, eligibility for marriage or transfer of wealth by inheritance. But the general similarity can be misleading. While the importance of "family" may be universal, ideals and even the definition of that term can differ considerably. The Roman word *familia*, for instance, usually means "household" or even "the slaves of the household." Latin does not have a word that clearly refers to what we today call the (nuclear) family. As a result, the shape of Roman family law can be surprisingly different from modern versions. For instance, it has very little to say about issues like grounds for divorce, alimony, child support, and child custody. In some instances this is because the Romans thought the questions were easier to answer than we do; in other cases, it is because they didn't ask the same questions in the first place. Other issues, such as the authority of a father over his adult children or treatment of dowry, loomed much larger in Rome than they do today. Over time, the shape of the Roman family (and of marriage in particular) changed. It was affected by several factors. One of the most dramatic of these was the rise of Christianity. The final section will look at the legal consequences of that transformation. (Some major aspects of the family and of family law have already been treated in Chapter 15 on inheritance, especially the rules of intestate succession. I will not repeat that material here.)

MARRIAGE AND DIVORCE

There were a number of requirements for marriage under Roman law. The parties had to be of opposite sexes and otherwise unmarried. They had to be Roman citizens, or have been granted the right of intermarriage (*conubium*) individually or as a member of a politically favored non-Roman community. (Roman law did not claim that noncitizens were unmarried; it just left that judgment to others.) They could not be close biological relatives; the formal definition in most cases was that they had to be at least five degrees (see Chapter 15) apart. And some closer step-relatives and in-laws were also prevented from marrying. They had to be of minimum reproductive age. Originally, this seems to have been regarded as a question of fact, to be determined on a case-by-case basis. Over time, the law shifted to a more standardized requirement of age twelve for girls and fourteen for boys. (Except for girls of the elite classes, the typical age of actual marriage appears to have been considerably higher than the legal minimum, though would-be marriages at even earlier ages are attested as well.) The elderly and the apparently infertile were generally allowed to marry, though castrated men were excluded. Finally, legislation of the emperor Augustus forbade marriage between those of very different social statuses, and these rules were somewhat extended by later emperors. Divorced people and widow(er)s were legally free to remarry, though a widow too quick to remarry would be viewed with suspicion socially. Serial marriage must have been quite common given ancient life expectancies, the common age gaps between husbands and wives, and the ease of Roman divorce.

The central and distinctive requirement for marriage, however, was simply agreement by both parties to be married. It is particularly noteworthy that consent was sought even from people (women, children in power) whose decision-making authority was restricted in other respects. If one or the other party was still in power, the consent of the father(s) was necessary *in addition*, but it could not substitute for the consent of the actual bride and groom.

In modern societies, marriage has a large number of automatic legal consequences, such as in taxation, private insurance, inheritance, citizenship, billing, and travel documentation. One group has counted over 1,400 of these in the United States. In Roman law, most of these did not exist. Still, there were several legal reasons it was important to know whether or not two people were married. Official terminology described marriage as "for the sake of producing children," and one of its principal legal effects was making children born (or at least conceived) within marriage legitimate. This in turn meant that the children inherited their father's Roman citizenship and gained qualified rights to inherit his property (Chapter 15). It also meant that they were subject to his *patria potestas* until his death. Children born outside a Roman marriage took their mother's citizenship (with certain exceptions), and their inheritance claims were limited on her estate and nonexistent on his. Their father did not have *patria potestas* over them. In fact, the law recognized no ties between illegitimate children and their biological fathers except to forbid them from marrying. Marriage also served to legitimize sexual behavior. Broadly speaking, Roman law forbade sex between unmarried persons unless the female partner was a prostitute or member of another officially disreputable class. Conversely, Imperial law penalized citizens of reproductive age who remained celibate for too long, and marriage was a way to avoid these penalties. (Those with enough children were exempt from staying married and were offered other small rewards.) Marriage also had effects, if limited ones, on property. Gifts between husband and wife were illegal (Chapter 16). When a marriage ended, it triggered the return of the dowry. As noted earlier (Chapters 10, 16), marriage did not give a husband control over his wife's property. Nor did the Romans recognize more egalitarian forms of "community property," nor did either spouse acquire any of the other's obligations. Two spouses could co-own property in exactly the same way as could any two unrelated people (Chapter 13), but their marriage (or divorce) had no effect on the joint ownership. Neither party could exercise anything like the kind of guardianship of an incapacitated spouse that we have today or otherwise act as a stand-in. Inheritance rights between spouses were weak and for a long time actually non-existent (Chapter 15). Marriage did have a few miscellaneous consequences that are better thought of as stemming from other parts of the law, not from marriage law itself. For instance, if a wife was slandered, her husband could sue for damages himself (Chapter 18). Starting from the time of the first emperor, unmarried persons were at a significant disadvantage in inheritance, and even once married, childless couples might not be allowed to inherit from each other. Outside of inheritance most of these circumstances, however, would arise only rarely.

The central role of consent makes Roman marriage look much like a contract (Chapter 12), but in one respect marriage law goes even further than contract law. Once contracts were agreed to, they were binding on both parties unless they were cancelled by *mutual* agreement. Marriage, however, ended if and when the consent ended on *either* side. Either spouse could divorce the other at any time and for any reason. Side agreements not to divorce or even to penalize the party who initiated a divorce were invalid. (There was one significant exception. A freedwoman could not divorce her patron-husband without his consent.)

This, at any rate, was the theory. While legally clear, the situation presented practical difficulties. First, it could be remarkably hard to prove the existence or absence of consent. Suppose you just act "single" by living alone or the like? Or even marry someone else? Second, technically, even transient breakdowns might end a marriage, even if neither spouse desired that in the long run. Imagine one partner running out of the house, shouting "I wish I'd never met you," only to return the next day. Is it really better to imagine this as two marriages separated by a twelve-hour divorce than to look the other way and ignore the possible break? Third, the tight focus on consent ignored any interest the other spouse or the community at large might have had in giving some stability to marriage. If marriage is meant to have any value beyond keeping track of the children (and all the evidence suggests that it did for the Romans), then its potential fragility must have been seen as a problem. There were traditional phrases and forms to divorce, and the law encouraged the use of these, even if it did not actually require them. (For some late exceptions, see the discussion that follows.) Still, the basic matter was so clear that there were no divorce cases, as such, in court; anyone desiring a divorce was by that very fact divorced. A court deciding some other matter (say, the inheritance of a disputed child) might have to rule in passing on *whether* or *when* a divorce had already taken place, but no government institution was needed to create the divorce in the first place or to resolve the related matters we typically associate with divorce today. Since the two parties had separate property during the marriage, there was no general need for any special settlement at the time of the divorce. Of course, a court might have to decide factual questions of who owned what in the first place. Neither party could claim alimony or any share of the other's future income. (Custody of children will be discussed later.)

Before moving on, it is worth noting that there is evidence for a more conservative phase earlier in Roman history. During the archaic period, it appears that only a husband could initiate divorce, and that he was expected to do so only because of moral "failings" on his wife's part. Divorce for insufficient reasons led to financial penalties for the husband. Roman legend traces the change in the classical system of free divorce (as described earlier) to a particular case in about 230 BC in which the divorcing husband got away without penalty, and new safeguards were felt to be needed. All the details of the story are suspect, but it does suggest that the change from the archaic system occurred quite early.

As with divorce, so with the marriage itself; there were certain customary forms that were not legally required for legitimacy, but which had some legal significance. "Betrothal" (a formal engagement) was not required but seems to have been customary, at least among some classes. Technically, the agreement was between the would-be spouses, but in practice the parents (when alive) seem to have been closely involved. Betrothed persons were treated as married for certain purposes (e.g., killing your betrothed's father was "parricide," aggravated familial murder), and this tendency grew over time. The engagement itself, however, was not enforceable, emphasizing again the importance of consent to Roman ideas of marriage. Dowry has already been mentioned, and though it was clearly not required for a valid marriage, it seems to have been so common as to be a good indicator of the intent to marry. There were conventional forms of wedding, most notably a formal procession from the bride's old home to her husband's, but again, none was required. It was even possible to marry an absent man if he sent agreement by messenger.

EXTRAMARITAL AFFAIRS

A married Roman woman was forbidden to have sex with anyone but her husband; to do so was called adultery. Originally this was grounds for divorce and loss of dowry (and a cause of grave social embarrassment). An adulterous wife caught in the act might often be killed, though the legal status of this revenge was not clear. Later, under the Empire, adultery became a public, criminal offense. Vigilante justice was actually restrained, but a conviction of the wife in court resulted in a combination of punishments including formal disgrace and fines.

Roman men were much freer. They were entitled to sexual relations with a variety of lower-status women (including, but not limited to, prostitutes and their own slaves) whether or not they were married. A man could be tried for adultery only for having sex with another man's wife, not merely because he was cheating on his own. A man might also form a more permanent union with a single women to whom he was not married, called a concubine. In many cases this was done because actual marriage was legally impossible, and sometimes, apparently, because the woman's social status was simply too low. A concubine had to be of marriageable age, and it was impossible to have both a wife and a concubine or multiple concubines at once. The main difference from marriage seems to have been that any offspring born from the relationship were illegitimate (see the next section) and therefore not legally their father's children.

CHILDREN

The most important facts about the legal position of children have already been treated in the discussion of *patria potestas* (Chapter 10). This section will take up some of the important remaining issues. In discussing *patria potestas*, we noted the largely unlimited power (in theory) of a father over the person and would-be property of his children in power. In this context, it is perhaps less surprising how little obligation a father (or, for that matter, a mother) had toward his or her child. Children were, as a matter of law, not that much different from slaves, though in practice they were normally treated far differently. There is no evidence of a parental obligation to support children before the second century AD. But the most striking fact to a modern eye is probably the practice of infant exposure. If a father did not wish a newborn to be raised, he could order it to be cast out, whether to die or to be picked up by someone else and raised (typically as a slave). Suspected motives for this include doubts about paternity, rejection of disabled children, and financial difficulties (especially in the case of girls), but we have very little idea how common any of these motivations (or indeed the practice in general) was. It is clear, however, that exposure was not thought of as a use of the theoretical and specially Roman "power of life and death" (Chapter 10); it remained legally uncontroversial long after execution of grown children was finally banned outright.

The same kind of thinking made questions of custody mostly trivial. At least originally, no court was needed to make fine judgments about the "best interests of the child." Legitimate children were their father's, and in the case of divorce he had the power to assign them as he saw fit. This, incidentally, may have discouraged women from seeking divorces to which they were legally entitled. Interdicts (see Chapter 13 on property) were available to make other parties, including the mother, produce the children. Stepmothers were important (and feared) figures in the world of the Roman imagination; the generic stepfather barely exists. As a matter of practice it may have been common to leave children, especially very young ones, with their mothers, but this was at the father's sufferance. Illegitimate children would in theory have been largely under the control of their guardians until reaching the age of majority, though our knowledge of actual practice here is weak. An Imperial decision of the mid second century AD did permit material custody, but only in extreme cases of bad paternal behavior and only (apparently) if the mother already had practical custody. This was perhaps originally a special case, but in the Empire, maternal custody became somewhat more common. Notwithstanding the general rules just stated, however, it should be noted that even asking about "custody" probably distorts the question somewhat. Roman law was probably more interested in maintaining the father's ownership rights and the children's inheritance rights than in the day-to-day maintenance of the children. So, for instance, there does not seem to have been a strong mechanism for recovering a child who had run away on her own.

The children we have been speaking of were normally the biological offspring of the parents in question, but in principle one could gain or lose parents by purely legal acts. Roman law recognized adoptions, and in practice they seem to have been accepted without the social ambivalence sometimes shown today. Romans typically adopted to provide an heir for the family. Hence, they adopted adults (safer in a world of high infant mortality) and males only (women would not continue the family name). At least among the elite, the adoptees were typically of similar status; there was no element of charity involved in this practice, except on the part of the "donating" family, whose own prospects of succession were at least a little harmed. The adopted child was entirely severed from his original family in terms of *patria potestas*, inheritance, and the rest (though some symbolic traces of the old family were generally retained, such as part of his old name). His rights and responsibilities in his new family were precisely those of a biological child. The other major motivation for adoption was one that no longer exists. A child born into slavery was not legally part of his biological family, even if subsequently freed. This situation could be (partially) corrected if the father went on to adopt the child; for technical reasons, however, this could be done only for a son. Daughters remained legal orphans. Moreover, the adoption tied the children only to the father, not to his wife (even if she were the biological mother).

Conversely, a child, like a slave, could be "emancipated." Such a child was thus freed from *patria potestas*. Originally, she was removed from her birth family as if she had never been part of it. Over time, however, emancipated children were allowed to retain certain rights, such as inheritance (Chapter 15). More precisely, they were allowed to claim a share of intestate inheritance, so long as they added their own estate to be distributed to their siblings. This was to make up for the "head start" they had at building up personal wealth. Roman fiction speaks often of "repudiation" of disobedient children, but this is not an actual term of law. Real emancipation need not result in disinheritance, and in fact seems usually to have been done as a favor to the child. It freed him from the oppression of *patria potestas* without automatically harming his position in any way.

CHRISTIANITY

The "Christianization" of the Roman Empire could have been expected to have had any number of effects on the broader law and society, and in fact many modern observers have claimed to have detected these. Some of the purported Christian influences are not ultimately convincing. Some reductions in the severity of punishments for slaves, for instance, are probably in large part the result of power struggles over who (private owner or state) was allowed to inflict those punishments. In family law, however, the Christian influence is somewhat clearer and more immediate. It is also true that "Christian" attitudes at the time were very much in flux. And in some instances, changes in law parallel or extend trends that had already come into being; but even then, Christianity pushed change further and faster. The most plausible cases of Christian influence are three. The penalties for the celibate established by the emperor Augustus were abolished by Constantine, the first Christian-influenced emperor. He also ended the tradition of free, unilateral divorce, outside of cases of grave fault. It should be noted, however, that after Constantine's drastic change the rules shifted frequently between the two extremes over the next two centuries. Also, contrary to what one might have expected from Christian texts, divorce by mutual consent remained unchanged. Constantine also eliminated execution of children by their fathers, though this seems to have vanished in practice long before. In Chapter 15, we noted a shift in inheritance law from seeing the "family" in terms of chains of fathers and sons to an emphasis on the nuclear family. This shift continued under the Christian emperors, but not for obviously religious reasons.

18. DELICT

❖❖❖❖❖❖❖❖❖

R OMAN AND COMMON LAW have similar ideas of a "wrongful act which does not involve a breach of contract and for which the injured party can recover damages in a civil action"; we call this a "tort," and in Roman law the parallel category of acts is called "delict." Delicts were tried according to private procedure, and the plaintiff, if successful, received money compensation for the damage but potentially also additional cash as a punishment of the wrongdoer. Thus delicts and torts are somewhere between crimes (very much the business of the state) and, say, contract disputes (primarily a matter between the parties alone). The main difference between tort and delict is that the Romans included under the heading of delict several offenses (theft, most assaults) that we routinely treat as crimes today. The following sections will treat three of the most important delicts, but I will begin by noting some features that are common to most or all of them. First, every delict required both an overt act and the intent to commit that act (even if not all the consequences were intended). Thus mere accident or bad intention alone could not give rise to a delict. These rules are shared with those for crimes (see the next chapter) as against, say, cases of contract law. Also (and again in common with the criminal law), not only the criminal himself was liable, but also persons who gave significant aid in planning or carrying out the action, so long as they too had the same intent, and all the participants in the act were individually liable for the full amount of damages. The criminal's heirs, however, were not liable, as they would have been in, say, a contractual matter.

DAMNUM INIURIA DATUM
(PROPERTY DAMAGE)

Damnum iniuria datum ("damage wrongfully done") is the subject matter of a delict originally defined by a mid-Republican statute called the *lex Aquilia*. Originally, the reach of the statute was limited to certain kinds of property damage. It applied to the killing of a slave or herd animal and to the "burning, breaking, or rending" of any property not covered by the killing provision. Over time, however, the jurists "interpreted" the statute so as to cover damage to essentially any property by any means. The remaining limitations can generally be seen as stemming directly from the definition. "Damage" (*damnum*) required both physical harm and loss of market value. Thus injury to a slave was covered, but personal injury to a free person (who had no cash value to start with) was not. Damage that did not reduce value was not covered – for example, castration of slaves or of animals not destined for breeding would not hurt (and might even increase) their market value. Nor was loss of value not based on physical damage covered – for example, spreading rumors about a competitor's product didn't break anything and so didn't count. "Wrongly" was taken to imply some responsibility beyond mere causation. Though the idea was not expressed this abstractly, the standard seems to have been that, assuming no malicious intent to harm another's property, the person doing the damage had only to exercise a "reasonable" level of care in protecting others' property from foreseeable harm to avoid a charge. Finally, "done" was taken to imply a reasonably direct form of causation, though in extremely indirect cases it would be hard to prove "wrongness" anyway.

The court trying a case of this sort had to decide not only whether the defendant was liable or not, but also the value of the damage done. There were two possibilities for what damages would then be awarded. If the defendant admitted liability at the beginning of the trial, the court would calculate the damages and charge him that amount. If he denied liability and was defeated at trial, the plaintiff would be awarded double damages. This possibility illustrates a significant difference between delicts and commercial matters like suits over contracts. In the latter case, the court simply tried to put things right by making the parties live up to their obligations. In cases of delict, there may also be a penalty over and above the restitution. In the case of the *lex Aquilia*, that penalty could be avoided by partial confession and so is a spur to peaceful dispute resolution. For some of the other delicts there were unavoidable penalty payments. In these instances, it is clear that the state was not just arbitrating between two private parties (in awarding actual damages), but stepping in to enforce its own values and discourage certain kinds of behavior (by the additional penalty).

You did not need to be the actual owner to have an action under this heading. Anyone with a formal financial interest could sue for such damages – for instance, the holder of a usufruct in some piece of property, or the holder of a pledge given as security, or even, say, a dry cleaner holding a customer's clothing. In the last case, the cleaner had legal responsibility to her customer to safeguard the clothing, and so could take action against a third party who damaged it. The same notion of interest also applies to the next delict, that of theft.

FURTUM (THEFT)

Theft originated as a private law matter in Roman law, rather than as the criminal offense we make of it today. If someone stole something from you, you had to detect and sue them. It involved not just the taking of something without the owner's permission, but the illegitimate use or "handling" of it. This included the embezzlement of items that were originally in your possession legitimately and even the "repurposing" of such items. For instance, if you kept a rental item beyond the agreed terms or used a rental car as a taxi (when you had agreed to personal use only), you might be liable for theft. Unlike many modern definitions, however, the scope of *furtum* did not include taking by fraud. This very broad "handling" definition made it important to be able to decide exactly what was being stolen. So, for instance, it was sometimes argued that if you took a single glass of wine from a cask, you had handled and therefore stolen the whole cask. By contrast, it was argued that you did not steal the cabinet you broke into to get at jewelry inside on the grounds that you didn't have the intent to steal it. Frankly, these various definitions and the relationships among them were never entirely worked out.

The specific damages awarded depended on a variety of circumstances. In the basic case, the thief had to pay double. There was a procedure that permitted a search of another's property to look for stolen goods, and there was a triple penalty if the goods were found in this way. Refusal of this search, theft by violence, and theft when the thief was caught in the act were penalized by quadruple payment. Note that the action on the delict would get you only this penalty payment in cash; a separate action would be required to get the actual object back. The whole system is problematic, at least in classic cases of theft, because professional thieves often fence property quickly and have few traceable assets. It does, however, still work to discourage embezzlement or repurposing. Still, under the Empire a criminal penalty was eventually developed.

INIURIA

This is perhaps the most complex of the delicts and almost certainly the one with the most complex evolution. The Twelve Tables made provisions for physical injury done to human beings. More serious injuries cost more than less serious ones, and injuries to free persons more than injuries to slaves. The latter provision partially overlapped with the eventual scope of the *lex Aquilia*, but the former was independent. In the mid second century BC, the scope of the delict was substantially expanded by the Edict. The story preserved for us is that a man walked through the Forum slapping passers-by and then voluntarily paying the statutory fine. Whether true or not, the story illustrates two important points. First, the statutory fines were fixed amounts that, over time, had been rendered largely obsolete by inflation. Second, the man's offense was not really physical harm (except incidentally), but the indignity suffered by his victims. The Edict addressed both issues. It allowed judges in individual cases to set appropriate penalties. It also allowed suits for any insult, whether attached to a physical injury or not. While the new scope of the delict was deliberately broad, there were certain areas that remained especially important.

The first of these was the original core area of physical assault, though any attack was now covered, not just one that did significant injury. The new version of *iniuria* now also covered defamation, whether in speech or in writing. Insulting songs may perhaps have been actionable before, under a different provision of the Twelve Tables, but even if so, that would have been rendered obsolete under the Edict. Beyond verbal defamation, other acts that might bring a person's reputation into question could also give rise to an *iniuria* action. For instance, there could be an action if someone falsely advertised another's property for a bankruptcy sale, or harassed them in mourning clothes (a traditional protest of unfair treatment), or if a man accosted a woman too familiarly in a public place. Finally, *iniuria* could involve preventing a person from exercising legal rights, even when this did not involve damage to person or reputation – for instance, if you prevent me from fishing in public waters or walking on public land.

Once the focus of *iniuria* shifted from physical injury to insult, it opened up the possibility of *iniuria* being done to one person by way of an action directed at another. So, for instance, *iniuria* to a woman was also an insult to her husband, and *iniuria* to a child in power was also an insult to his or her father. In all these cases, all the actions could be available simultaneously. So, for instance, if a man harasses a woman in a way that calls her chastity into question, she can sue for *iniuria*. But the same man has simultaneously called into question the honor of her husband and father (if any), and so they can sue as well, and damages can be awarded independently in all three cases.

Moreover, it was possible to commit *iniuria* against someone through a slave. A certain amount of rough treatment of slaves (anyone's slaves) was taken for granted, but "too much" such treatment showed disrespect for the owner. The slave had no action of his own, but the owner could sue. It was even possible for an heir to sue over outrage to the corpse of the person from whom she had inherited (and whom she was therefore charged to honor).

Some of the cases just mentioned also illustrate another important feature of *iniuria* law. Because the basic idea is so tied up with personality and reputation, *iniuria* reflects a wider variety of cultural values (and some of the most Roman-specific ones) than other areas of law. So, for instance, it is clear that a woman's reputation was normally thought of in terms of her reputation for chastity. Interestingly, the same seems to have been true for youths of either sex. Adult men, on the other hand, were not thought to be insulted by implications that they were sexually aggressive or available. Another point about gender is made by the rules for derivative *iniuria*. Men could be insulted by actions against related women, but the reverse did not hold. Men had broader responsibility (a fact that they used in turn to justify greater authority). *Iniuria* law also makes explicit other kinds of social hierarchy. Under a variety of circumstances the court could find that an act of *iniuria* was especially offensive (*atrox*). One of these circumstances involved *iniuria* done to a person of distinguished social rank by a person of lower rank. In the American law of defamation, the famous have *less* protection for various reasons, among them the idea that these people can defend themselves. The Roman law reflected the opposite view: these people had more reputation to lose, and so their loss was worth more.

19. CRIMES AND PUNISHMENTS

❧❧❧❧❧❧❧❧❧

T HE ROMAN COURTS divided cases into the "private" and
"public" in something like the way we divide "civil" and
"criminal." One of the important differences is that in Roman
law some of our main criminal offenses (most thefts and assaults,
seemingly including murder) were in the private category for
most of our period. The public offenses also attracted much less
attention from the Roman jurists than private-law matters, and
surviving speeches from actual prosecutions have surprisingly
little to say about legal issues. The explanation for all these
facts may be that the Romans had a very political understanding of the role of the public courts. This is not to say that they
were "political" in a corrupt sense (though that might be true
as well). Rather, they existed only to treat matters that were
inherently political in that they affected the community as a
whole (say, electoral bribery or abuse of office). An offense to
an individual victim with no broader consequences, no matter
how heinous, just was not the right *kind* of offense for these
courts. Mere law and order were not sufficient grounds. And
to the extent that the community was defending itself in these
courts, the law was not acting as a fair or impartial third party

settling disputes. Hence, lawyers were neither interested or interesting in these contexts. In the rest of this chapter I will speak of "crime(s)" for convenience, but keep in mind that I really mean "public-law offense," and that this is something slightly different.

Before discussing particular procedures and offenses, I will point out a few general principles of criminal liability. Most of these, as we saw in the last chapter, applied to delict as well. These rules were formalized later than the individual offenses (if at all), but they seem to have been generally observed even earlier. Committing a crime always involved an overt act. You could not be convicted for omission or for mere bad intentions. Intention, however, was important. Accidental and reckless action was not sufficient for a crime to have been committed; you had to have actual intent. So drunken brawlers were not to be treated as murderers, even if someone died in a fight. Finally, as long as someone committed the actual crime, other people could also be convicted if they were loosely attached. The standard phrase is "anyone by whose plan or effort" the crime was committed.

REPUBLICAN PROCEDURES

There were no separate criminal courts until quite late in Roman history; the first was created in 149 BC, and this only tried a single offense. Before this, major public offenses (e.g., treason, misuse of state funds) were tried before assemblies of the whole (voting) population – the same groups that passed laws and elected magistrates. Charges were brought by various magistrates, and sentences typically included fines and/or exile. On a few occasions in the second century BC, this elaborate procedure was replaced by an investigatory commission led by a major magistrate and authorized in some cases by vote of the people and in some cases by the Senate. This was done only on an individualized, ad hoc basis, and the legality of the whole procedure was not clear.

Beginning in the middle of the second century BC, trials before the assemblies began to be replaced more systematically by a procedure (the so-called *quaestio perpetua* or "standing inquiry") that looked much more like the kind of trial we are used to, though it was still close in some respects to a private process. A separate court was established to try each offense, so there were slight procedural differences among them, though the details are not important here. There was no district attorney, crown prosecutor, or other state agent. Prosecutions had to be launched by private citizens, though the prosecutor need not have been a victim of, or even connected to, the crime. The would-be prosecutor went to the praetor to ask permission to proceed, though we do not know how often this was denied. If more than one person wished to prosecute, then a preliminary hearing was held in which the jury had to decide which party would do a better job of arguing the main case. The jurors were selected from a panel of rich and merely well-to-do citizens (the precise rules of eligibility were the subject of much political dispute) by a process of alternating rejections by the two sides. The end result was a panel of roughly twenty-five to seventy-five jurors (and, ideally, an odd number). The hearing of a case proceeded in much the same way as a private case: long speeches followed by witness testimony and other evidence. Both sides were typically represented by advocates. There was little intervention by the government in terms of admissible evidence, subpoenas (in most cases), discovery, and so forth. And not only was there no detailed charge to the jury (the elaborate legal instructions given by a judge today), but there was not even a formula of the sort given in Roman private cases. At the end of the trial, the jurors did not deliberate but simply voted, and a majority vote won. There was no appeal from their verdict.

REPUBLICAN OFFENSES

The system of the standing inquiries came to try seven offenses: electoral bribery, provincial extortion, homicide, riot, forgery, theft of public property, and treason. Full definitions and punishments will be listed later. Two general points about penalties need to be made first. Several of the offenses carried a "capital" penalty. In theory, this might mean execution (as it does today), but in practice that punishment seems rarely or never to have been carried out on Roman citizens. Rather, they were allowed to slip into exile abroad (and possibly have their property confiscated). This way out is part of a broader pattern. None of the penalties for Roman citizens involved corporal punishment. Instead, those convicted of these offenses (as well as in some lesser, civil matters) suffered a variety of civic disabilities (e.g., a ban on office holding) called by the umbrella term *infamia*. There are a very few known exceptions, but these do not involve ordinary criminal offenses and even then were controversial among contemporaries.

Ambitus. This is electoral bribery. Buying votes directly was illegal from early on, but over time other forms of electoral malpractice were also included: giving out tickets to public games (or putting them on in the first place) or seats at feasts, making deals with other candidates to share votes, gathering an excessive entourage. The most immediate penalty was being disqualified from the election (only winners seem to have been prosecuted), but there was a further bar from seeking office for another decade. This was eventually strengthened to exile (perhaps with a limited term). At some point, the candidate's principal agents became specifically liable as well.

Repetundae. This offense is sometimes described as "extortion" from provincial subjects. (The Latin term means "recovery" and is properly the name of the court rather than of the crime itself.) The original scope of the offense seems to have been for a provincial governor to receive more than a specified amount of money from one of his subjects, whether as gift, bribe, "protection" money, or even otherwise legitimate payment. Over time, other forms of official misbehavior were included, such as taking bribes of any size, excessive requisitions from subjects (even for overtly public purposes), and (eventually) leaving one's own province without authorization (presumably on a military adventure). This offense had the most procedural peculiarities, most notably a provision to give Roman advocates to foreign plaintiffs, and some opportunity for the prosecution to subpoena witnesses. The penalty for the core offense was to pay back twice the amount taken, so there had to be a second hearing after a guilty verdict to establish the amount of damages.

Homicide. In early times, homicide seems to have been a criminal offense only under a few circumstances: using of poison, killing a near relative, and (later) having some connection to organized crime. The recognition of murder in general as an offense seems not to have happened until perhaps 81 BC. Even after this time, there seems to have been an emphasis on prosecutions for the kinds of killings just mentioned and for a fourth special type, so-called judicial murder, that is, the abuse of the criminal process to bring about someone's death. The punishment was "capital" in the sense described earlier.

Vis. The Latin name for this offense means simply "force" or "violence," but the scope of the crime seems to have been much narrower. Prosecutions for *vis* did not arise from just any use of violence (say, a tavern brawl or a mugging), but only from those that were "against the state." That is, the violence had to have a clear political aim or be on such a scale (a riot more than an assault) as to take on political implications. Over time, some individual acts seem to have been specified by the statute or by explanatory decrees of the Senate (e.g., seizing public places, stirring up the troops), but the basic definition remained abstract and vague. This meant it was subject to changes in public opinion, and in practice more and more acts were deemed "against the state" over time. The definition also lent itself to a utility defense. That is, a defendant might more or less admit the violence but claim that it was for the public good. The penalty was capital.

Falsum. The charge covered counterfeiting of coins and forgery of wills. The former offense was more narrowly defined than one might expect today. Nothing prevented persons from producing coinage in metals not used for the official currency. (Since money drew much of its value from its precious-metal content, this would not be a silly thing to do.) The penalty was capital.

Peculatus. While ordinary thefts were delictal matters, theft of state-owned property fell under this criminal category. A person who had legitimate possession of that property (at least initially) could not be charged with this offense, though he might be liable on other charges. The penalty was a combination of exile and restitution (the latter requiring a separate hearing to calculate the amount stolen).

Maiestas. Literally "majesty" or "greater-ness," the full name of this offense was "diminishing the majesty of the Roman people." Like the laws on *vis*, those on *maiestas* specified a (growing) number of particular acts, but both prosecution and defense could always fall back on the more abstract definition. It was a standard rhetorical exercise to argue how one's supposed acts of *maiestas* had actually increased the majesty of the Roman people. While the term is sometimes translated "treason," that is misleading. The main overlap is in cases where a magistrate is prosecuted for gross malpractice in military command and where there is perhaps an incidental suggestion that he may have been bribed by the enemy. Other acts that might be prosecuted as *maiestas* included interfering with a magistrate in the performance of his duties, waging war without proper authorization, and wasting state resources. The penalty was capital.

CHANGES UNDER THE EMPIRE

The most important change under the Empire was probably the collapse of most criminal jurisdiction into the *cognitio* procedure that was also coming into use for civil cases (Chapter 11). Just as in private law, this made the state much more activist than it had been. But the substantive effects of the change were much greater than they had been in private law. Since *cognitio* procedure was formally beyond the statutes that established the standing inquiries, it was not bound either by their definitions or by their penalties. While the old rules were not systematically thrown out, a substantially new system evolved. I will say more about the offenses later, but first we may note major changes in the range of penalties. First, while exile had been a way to escape execution, it now became a penalty in its own right. Depending on the specific offense, the exile might have more or less choice about where to go and might or might not have property confiscated. Second, physical punishments such as condemnation to forced labor and execution were established. Third, a two-tiered set of penalties was set up. Ordinary citizens (*humiliores*) were largely subject to the new corporal penalties, including aggravated forms of execution such as crucifixion. Elites (*honestiores*) were typically subject to fines or to the various forms of exile or (in extreme cases) to simple execution. At the very top of the social scale, the Senate began to sit as a court to try its own members whenever they were accused of criminal offenses.

In the early years of the Empire, two new statutory criminal offenses were added to the court system. One was adultery, defined as sex between a married woman and a man other than her husband. Both parties were equally guilty, but note that a married man could have sex with, say, a slave or prostitute without committing any legal offense at all. The penalty was a fine along with restrictions on remarriage, though much of the purpose of the law seems to have been to discourage injured parties from taking the law into their own hands. There was also a new crime of interfering with the public grain supply, punishable by a schedule of fines.

More important than these early statutory changes was a series of shifts and expansions within the *cognitio* procedure. As part of the freedom created by the new procedure, new offenses were created and particular acts were brought under the scope of previous offenses. So, for instance, arson and castration came to be prosecuted under what was nominally still the homicide statute. In some cases, this created considerable overlap. For instance, possession of a weapon with criminal intent could be tried under both the *vis* and homicide statutes.

Some entirely new offenses were created, such as kidnapping and rustling. The limitation of criminal *vis* to acts "against the state" was largely dropped (so this, for instance, was the heading under which rape would be prosecuted). And several of the delicts (e.g., theft, fraud, *iniuria*) were eventually criminalized. Finally, the scope of *maiestas* law was radically transformed. While its original scope was probably never redefined in theory, in practice it came quickly to focus on the person of the emperor. Depending on the political circumstances, almost any action that showed (or could be construed to show) disrespect for the emperor might bring about prosecution. (In this imperial sense, the translation of "treason" makes more sense.)

20. RELIGIOUS LAW

❖❖❖❖❖❖❖❖

THERE WAS NO IDEA in Rome of the "separation of church and state." During the earliest period of the Roman government, certain priesthoods were the guardians and arbiters of the law. Even after this period, many priesthoods remained state offices; there were many public rituals; and public money was spent on religious buildings and the like. And many have noted the markedly legal cast of Roman religion itself. Rituals, prayers, and responses to prodigies had to take prescribed forms. The "pontiffs" who had originally been guardians of the law in general remained less "priests" in the modern sense than religious lawyers. Hence it is not surprising that religious law was one of the major subcategories of public law in Rome. But other factors limited the reach of religious law. First, on the legal side of things, is the mere fact that divine law was, after that archaic period, a *sub*category of public law. The gods, apparently, did not have preferences in most mortal matters, and humans were left to their own devices in these areas. Second, on the divine side, religious authority was decentralized, and orthodoxy was not, in most respects, a Roman goal. Not even clearly religious activity in private homes, for instance, seems to have been of much interest to the authorities. There was some interest in preserving the existence of familial rites, perhaps especially the maintenance of ancestor worship, but there were no uniform regulations for the specific content. Moreover, what clear and specific rules did exist even outside the family often governed the practice of local cultic activity, the equivalent today of, say, rules on how to say mass in a single Catholic church: who could hold particular priesthoods and what taboos they faced, how to perform certain sacrifices, how to dispose of a god's property. In this chapter, I will not treat rules that are strictly about ritual practice. Rather, I will point out the narrow respects in which religious law could impinge on the human world.

SACRED THINGS

According to Roman law, property could be subject to "human" or "divine" law, though of course both kinds of law told human beings, not gods, what to do. The divine law offered up two different important kinds of sacred objects (there was also a third type, but we can safely ignore it). What all the types share is the idea that an object subject to divine law is no longer available for human sale, gift, or even ownership. If formerly ordinary property became sacred, the owner's interest and all associated rights (such as servitudes; see Chapter 14) were extinguished. Where the types differ, at least in theory, is primarily in *how* an object comes to be sacred. The first important type is called *sacer* (I will use the Latin terms here, since English has no parallel way of talking about three different kinds of "sacred"ness). These are objects that have been dedicated to, and thus become the property of, specific heavenly divinities. They might include temples and the land on which they sat, statuary, or any items given as sacrifices. Such dedications were typically made by governmental action, or at the least had to be authorized in general terms by the state. A famous case from the late first century BC will illustrate the potential difficulties here. When Cicero was sent into exile in 58, his property was confiscated by the state (as was normal in cases of exile). His archenemy Clodius apparently foresaw that the exile would not be permanent, and so he seized control of Cicero's house in downtown Rome and had a temple dedicated to the goddess Liberty on the site. When Cicero was restored in the following year, most of his property was also returned to him. Clodius, however, tried to block the return of the house on the grounds that it was no longer subject to human control, and so the authorities had no right to dispose of it. A series of hearings then took place over the next year before the Senate and involving at least two bodies of priests. Cicero argued that there were numerous technical flaws in the dedication, and that it was thus invalid. He never, however, disputed the premise. If the property was "really" dedicated to the goddess, then it was gone.

The other major kind of sacred property is very different. This (called *religiosus*) was land used for human burial, and it became sacred by virtue of the burial itself, so long as it was carried out by an authorized person. (You can't make your neighbor's land *religiosus* by sneaking over and burying your late uncle there.) Naturally, there were disputes among the lawyers about just what constituted "burial" and who was "authorized," but the major problem with this kind of land is more basic. The legal sources all take for granted the general principle mentioned earlier and apparently confirmed for *sacer* property by the case of Cicero's house: sacred land is taken out of the world of human ownership and commerce. In fact, the principle was broadened somewhat. For technical reasons, land outside Italy could not be *sacer* or *religiosus*, but the legal and land-surveying texts assert that it was to be treated as such anyway. Yet in practice it seems to have been quite common to buy and sell tombs and especially to dispose of them by will. Nor was this some kind of secret black market. We know of the practice from, among other things, numerous inscriptions on the tombs themselves that attempted to control their transfer [20–22]. Various theories have been suggested to explain this, mostly variations on the idea that something other than the actual tomb was being owned, bought, sold, and so on, but no one has come up with a genuinely satisfying solution (see further the discussion in Chapter 22).

CHECKING WITH THE GODS

The Romans had a variety of devices for communicating with the gods – watching birds or lightning, observing the entrails of sacrificial animals, and occasionally reacting to random prodigies like the birth of a two-headed animal or a rain of stones. This communication was rarely aimed at prophecy in the sense of discovering the future. Rather, the goal was to discover divine judgment of a past or present action. Most of the time what was sought was a simple yes-or-no answer: did the gods approve of some government action? As with the notion of "sacred" property just discussed, this general idea took on somewhat different forms in different contexts, some of which are more relevant to the law than others.

Before holding an election or having the assembly vote on legislation, a magistrate had, at a minimum, to check for certain signs in the sky. Normally, this was done by the magistrate who would preside over the meeting, but in principle all the senior magistrates were competent to take notice of such omens. In addition to the supervising magistrates, who acted as the authorized representatives of the Roman people before the gods, there were standing bodies of priests who were supposed to be expert in the particular forms of omens. "Augurs" knew the sky signs, for instance, and "haruspices" were specialists in entrails. Moreover, signs of all sorts might be forwarded to the Senate for action, and the Senate might farm them back out to one or the other of the priestly bodies for study before taking action. The lack of clear rules meant that the interaction between religion and human law and legislation was not always predictable. Two examples may help to illustrate this.

While consul in 59, Julius Caesar often butted heads with the other consul, Bibulus. He even resorted to inciting mob violence to drive away his uncooperative colleague. Eventually, Bibulus gave up trying to intervene directly in the legislative process and instead shut himself up in his house, issuing periodic written statements that he was "watching the skies." This phrase meant that he was looking for omens and that (as everyone knew) he would "find" signs that disapproved of the assemblies. Caesar persisted anyway, and for years afterward the validity of the legislation passed during his term remained in some doubt. On the one hand, it could be argued that none of the assemblies in question had been properly authorized and so technically none of their laws were genuine. On the other hand, it might be argued that technically there had been no adverse omens, only a threat to look for them. The matter was never really resolved, largely for political reasons (no one wanted *all* of Caesar's laws overturned), but also because of the lack of a central authority on religious law. The other example takes us back to the case of Cicero's house mentioned earlier. When Cicero initially tried to recover his house, the Senate referred the matter to the most lawyerly priests, the pontiffs. On their recommendation, it was decided that there had been no proper dedication, and thus that Cicero would get his property back. But the following year some ambiguous omens led to a widespread belief that the gods were displeased with some recent action. Cicero's enemies suggested that they were displeased with the reoccupation of his land and were showing that the previous decision had been incorrect. The Senate referred the matter to a second set of religious experts, who produced a report nearly as ambiguous as the omens themselves, and the Senate eventually decided not to reverse itself.

A different set of religious authorities had a more specialized role in declaring war and making treaties. The so-called *fetiales* carried out rituals by which the Romans demanded restitution from other nations that had done them some harm and formally declared war when they (inevitably) refused it. We know that in this process they stressed the justice of the Roman cause, and the whole proceeding was framed much as a legal case between the Romans and their opponents, a case whose verdict would be revealed by the outcome of the war. They were also involved in striking treaties at the end of wars. While the priesthood was never abolished, its actual use seems to have become at most occasional by the period treated in this book. It is unfortunately unclear whether the role of the *fetiales* in this process gave them any power, even when they were formally involved. That is, was there an independent religious test of whether Rome could or should go to war, or did the *fetiales* essentially just file the correct paperwork with the gods?

THE POWER OF RELIGIOUS LAW

It is possible to read both of these stories as cases of human politics trumping religious law, but that is at best an oversimplification. What the "right" answer was in terms of religious law was hardly clear in either case, so politicians had a lot of room to maneuver. Thus it is worth noting the power of religious law in matters where its rules are clearer. So, for instance, the newly bought house of Titus Calpurnius Lanarius was destroyed around 100 BC on order of the augurs. It turned out that the structure blocked a sight line needed for taking certain auspices. Apparently, Calpurnius did not resist the ruling, but just had the house demolished. (He could and did, however, sue the seller for not revealing the hidden defect; see Chapter 12 on *bonae fidei* contracts.) The jurists conceded that it was the priests, not themselves, who could judge whether renovation of a tomb had shaded over into desecration or whether bodies once buried could be removed for reburial elsewhere (see [27]). And priests apparently had to approve adoptions (see Chapter 17) of persons who were in their own power. Apparently, this is because of the religious implications of the act itself. An independent person was the head of a family that presumably had family religious rites. The adoption would extinguish the family, and that would end the performance of the rites. Hence the need for priestly approval.

The issue is complicated by the fact that most of the power to make religious decisions was in the same (small) set of hands that also held political power. The Senate made decisions on a number of religious issues, and this may even have been a rare area in which they had direct (rather than advisory) authority. The priesthoods were nearly all held by members of the senatorial class, and most of these were actual holders of political office. When an individual who is both a politician and a religious official makes a decision in a case with both political and religious implications, it is impossible (on our evidence) to tell how the two kinds of issues interact. But at the least religious law had some force of its own. As we have noted, it could have force even against what would have been the normal civil law result in situations that were relatively nonpolitical. It is not impossible, then, that religious imperatives would have been respected even in politically sensitive situations.

At the same time, there were areas where we can see a retreat in religious law. There are areas in which it seems to have existed, but was later replaced by civil law. The most notable of these is inheritance. We are told that in the early days the pontiffs dictated the rules of inheritance, particularly with a view to linking property and rites. That is, the person who got the most benefit from the deceased's estate was also to bear the burden of keeping up the family sacrifices. Yet Cicero complained in the mid first century BC that the two kinds of succession had come apart. The jurists had taken over the inheritance of property, apparently leaving the sacred rites for the priests.

21. LAW IN THE PROVINCES

෯෯෯෯෯෯෯෯

MOST OF THIS BOOK has assumed that the persons involved in its situations were Romans living in Rome (or perhaps their slaves). Roman law, however, was fairly sensitive both to the citizenship of individuals and to the location of a given legal dispute. (Since one's birth citizenship rarely changed, citizenship and location often do not line up.) Thus we need to think at least a little about several other situations: Romans interacting with each other abroad, Romans and aliens interacting (both in Rome and elsewhere), and two non-Romans interacting within an area of Roman rule.

CITIZENSHIP AND JURISDICTION

The central principle is what we today call the "personality principle." That is, the law that governs you depends more on who you are than on where you are. Consider, for instance, an Athenian or Jewish couple living in Rome but without Roman citizenship. Were they legally married? What rights did they have against each other or any children? What happened to the property when one or the other died? The Roman law rules discussed earlier (Chapters 15 and 16) did not apply. Rather, the Romans left this up to Greek and Jewish law, respectively, to decide. (If there was no nearby court to decide these issues conveniently, that was not the Romans' problem.) Of course, there were exceptions to this principle, and these will be discussed later, but it is important to begin with one clarification. Limited jurisdiction is a legal concept, not a political one. If you are not subject to the local laws, this does not give you freedom; it means you are not protected by the laws. In particular, the local authorities can punish you in any way they see fit on any (or even no) grounds. There are a few known instances in which Roman authorities used that power in situations that created diplomatic problems. For instance, in the late second century BC, a Roman consul had the mayor of an Italian town beaten because the city baths had not been prepared quickly enough for the consul's wife. Even here, Rome was the final arbiter of its own convenience. The Italian had no legal recourse; at best, the Romans might be convinced that their fellow citizen's cruelty had made him a *political* liability.

However, breakdowns in the theoretical distinctions of the personality principle were both early and sometimes significant. While the statute law technically applied only to the citizens, the praetor could grant judgment in whatever other cases and to whomever he wished. Thus the creations of the Edict (say, the consensual contracts) were available to all. Moreover, a similar mechanism could extend much of the statute law to noncitizens; the praetor instructed judges to decide cases "as if" the parties were citizens. The timing and speed of these developments is unclear, but in 242 BC the Romans created a "peregrine" praetor. The role of this official is disputed, but his title shows that in some way he handled legal disputes involving noncitizens. The creation of a whole new office suggests that there were already many such cases. Access to parts of Roman law could also be extended to individuals or communities. The Latins had the right of intermarriage with Romans (*conubium*) as well as Roman property rights (*commercium*). Other Roman allies were sometimes awarded the same rights as early as the late third or early second century BC. Finally (if much more rarely), the Romans' superior political and military position allowed them simply to announce rules binding on their neighbors in matters such as the regulation of "foreign" religious associations and limits on interest rates.

LAW IN THE PROVINCES

The story I have been telling so far in this chapter has largely been set in Italy and was shaped by the peculiar political history of the Roman conquest of the rest of the peninsula. Over the course of the Republic, Rome claimed more and more territory throughout Italy and populated it with more and more Roman citizens. At the same time, however, half of Italy was left as more or less independent city-states bound to Rome by treaty rather than by absorption, and this state of affairs continued until early in the first century BC. As a result, there were many opportunities for Roman citizens to live and work with nearby citizens of numerous other communities, hence the need for expanded access to Roman law just described. In theory, some other uniform system for all Italy could have done just as well, but the Romans were vastly more powerful than any of the other remaining states, so naturally they were able to impose their own law as the principal solution. When, however, Rome moved out to conquer the Mediterranean basin and the rest of its eventual territory, the administration of the resulting empire was much different than it had been closer to home. When Romans conquered territory, they often established a permanent government there, sending governors who collected taxes and exercised final authority. Independent communities continued to exist in some places, as they had in Italy, and their people were clearly not Roman citizens, but they were in a much clearer position of subordination. Moreover, this meant that Romans had authority over disputes in which neither party was actually a Roman.

As a matter of legal theory, the simplest way to deal with this situation might have been the following: In disputes between two Romans, Roman law could be applied in normal fashion, with the provincial governor taking the place of the praetor. Disputes between two citizens of an alien community would continue to be resolved under their local law. In cases of mixed citizenship, the "right" solution is less clear, but there does seem to have been a general principle that a person was to be sued in his or her own place of residence; perhaps the rule could have been generalized to use the defendant's legal system as well. While this theory works as a very rough approximation of what actually happened, the situation was in fact much more complicated. First, while this solution is compatible with Roman legal theory, the Romans themselves seem not to have worked out such a specific theory of jurisdiction. Second, they seem in practice to have decided such questions as much (if not more) as political matters than as legal ones. The same legal dispute might have been handled in very different ways at different times, in different places, or with parties of different statuses. Rather than trying to give a complete set of rules here (which even the most advanced scholarship cannot do with the current evidence), I will offer a list of the most important variables.

- *The seriousness of the dispute.* Civil law matters were more likely to be left to local authorities than public (including criminal) ones. Among civil law cases, the Roman government was more likely to intervene in high-value cases than in lower-value ones. In several cases we know that specific values triggered a move from local courts to the higher provincial authority, but we also know that these values were not standardized from place to place. A larger town might be given more judicial authority than a smaller one nearby.
- *Local agreements.* Individual communities were sometimes granted special rights to manage their own legal affairs by treaty or by Roman decree. This was not specifically a matter of legal policy but a mark of political respect. A city that had proven particularly valuable to Rome, whether by general

good behavior, performance during some crisis, or services to an important Roman individual, was granted these rights as a sign of favor. In some cases individuals were given the right to choose under which system their cases would be decided.

• *Status of the participants.* A governor would be more likely to intervene in a case involving more important persons. In particular, he might step in (perhaps thereby imposing Roman law) in cases involving Roman citizens. He might even do so in contradiction of the kind of local agreements just discussed. For instance, the murder of a Roman citizen in his province was known to attract a governor's attention no matter what the formal arrangements.

• *Time and space.* Different provinces developed their own traditions, lasting beyond the terms of individual governors. At least in some cases these customs were treated as virtual laws, though it is unlikely that they were technically binding. That said, there was also a general trend across the empire to establish increasingly clear rules over time.

• *Substantive versus procedural law.* In principle, it would be possible for Roman procedures (e.g., the two-phase trial, the use of a formula) to be followed even if the substantive rules to be applied (hierarchies of intestate succession, say, or requirements for a valid contract) were local. In fact, there seem to be at least a few cases in which we know just this pattern was followed (e.g., "sacred" provincial land; see Chapter 20 and the following discussion). It has been suggested, though, that the principle applied much more generally than these few clear examples show. The nature of the Roman system would certainly lend itself to this. The governor could appoint a judge and give a (typically vague) formula in good Roman fashion, and the local *iudex* could then easily apply local law in the particular trial, and we might never be the wiser. We will see one possible case in the last section of this chapter, but most of the time the evidence does not really tell us whether procedure and substance went together.

• *Individual judgment.* The judgment (or the mere whim) of the Roman governor may have been the single most important factor in deciding how issues were resolved in his province. The desire to help personal friends (especially, but not necessarily, Romans) could draw him into a case; the desire to stay out of and above local squabbles might keep him out, as would a desire to limit his own workload. He might even have principled reasons to accept or avoid jurisdiction. If we can give a general rule, it might be this: While there was probably no circumstance in which a Roman governor felt he had no *right* to intervene in a case within his province, he ordinarily saw no *need* to do so, at least in cases without obvious political implications.

Nonetheless, there was a clear trend over time (beyond the move toward greater standardization), and this was in the direction of the increasing Romanization of all legal processes. This occurred for at least four reasons. First, as noted in Chapter 2, significant grants of Roman citizenship (and of the "halfway"

Latin status) were made from the end of the Republic on. Early on, these grants were typically made to individuals or small groups, but early in the first century BC the non-Roman parts of Italy were absorbed en masse, and under the Empire citizen status came to be given to whole communities and occasionally even to whole regions. Finally, in AD 212 an imperial decree made citizens of virtually all free inhabitants of the empire. In theory, this could have eliminated indigenous traditions of non-Roman law instantly, though we will see later that things were not actually so simple.

Second, Roman political authorities increasingly used their own law to settle disputes in which the two parties were not both from the same foreign state, and so there was no (single) "foreign" system to follow — for example, cases between a Roman and a provincial, between provincials from two different cities, and cases including persons from outside the empire entirely. We also know of cities that decided minor cases themselves, but had to refer more important matters to the Roman authorities.

Third, even communities that retained formal judicial independence sometimes changed their laws to resemble those of Rome, especially in the western half of the empire. This conformity seems to have been encouraged but not required by the central government.

Finally, the losing party in any dispute might appeal to Roman authority just to have a second chance to win. In these last two instances, subjects and subject states colluded in weakening their own legal systems.

FOREIGN EFFECTS ON ROMAN LAW

Most of the discussion so far in this chapter has been about *choosing* legal systems. Will a Roman or non-Roman court hear a particular case? Will that court follow Roman or local legal traditions? Who gets to decide? These kinds of sharp either/or distinctions seem to be typical of the interaction between Roman law and other legal systems, but things did not always work that way. There are also cases where we can see combinations and modifications of multiple systems. In general, this seems to have been more a matter of practice than of theory. That is to say, Roman officials and jurists rarely admitted outside influence, but documents of individual transactions in the real world show clear traces of it. Now, given this mismatch between theory and practice, we do not know how successful the hybrid forms were. Perhaps parties who tried to use partially "foreign" law were laughed out of Roman courts. But there are enough examples in the records of experienced users of the law to suggest that at least some bits of non-Roman law established a place for themselves among the Romans. Because of the general lack of recognition of foreign law in Roman texts, it is hard to give a general account. Instead, I will discuss four concrete examples.

My first two examples are also among the few where "official" sources are illuminating: rules for burial and surveillance of pregnant women. Both cases are relatively simple in that they involve transfer of large blocks of law at once. As we saw in Chapter 20, Roman law observed several categories of land subject to "the legal authority of the gods" and generally not subject to human buying and selling. A legal textbook points out that only land in Italy could technically be "sacred" or "religious," but adds that provincial land that would otherwise qualify for one of these statuses was "treated as" sacred or religious. We happen to have some confirming information a little closer to the ground. A handbook for surveyors mentions these same categories of land in a way that explicitly raises the issue of Italian versus provincial land. Interestingly, here the location of the parcel of the land was important for practical rather than for theoretical reasons. Italian land was more densely settled, and so it was more likely that neighbors might start to encroach on sacred places. The legal textbook says to ignore the technicality; the surveying manual does ignore it entirely. But if we treat "sacred" land as if it were genuinely sacred, that does not tell us which land counts as "sacred" in the first place. Roman religious rules were very place-specific, so there were no standards to universalize, even if the authorities had wanted to do so. Perhaps, then, if the locals recognized some place as sacred by their *own* standards, Roman law would kick in, and its protections would apply. This general rule is never actually attested, but in at least one specific case (reburial after a flood) we have an imperial pronouncement that local custom may substitute for the judgment that would have been rendered by the religious authorities in Rome [27]. There is also evidence of a similar substitution of rules regarding surveillance of pregnant women. The Edict laid out a remarkably elaborate set of procedures to track a widow's pregnancy and ensure that any posthumous child of her late husband was in fact his. Yet at the end of a long discussion of the rules, the jurist Ulpian says that in the interests of fairness to the child, his or her legitimacy should not be compromised if alternative local procedures are used. Again, Roman law sets the big question, but allows local law to provide the answer.

For a somewhat different relationship between Roman and foreign (in this case Greek) law, we can look to the role of something called *arra* (or *arrabo*) in the law of sale. The term refers to a kind of deposit or earnest money; the buyer put down some of the price up front at the making of the contract, and the rest later (say, at delivery of the merchandise). Roman law never required such a deposit. A sale became binding on the mere agreement of the parties (Chapter 12). Even if the buyer did offer it, its only legal function was to serve as evidence of a seriously intended contract (and perhaps of the price). The closest thing in Roman law would perhaps be a forfeiture clause, requiring a buyer to pay a penalty if the deal were not concluded in a specified time. Yet there is considerable evidence of the long-term popularity of the device in Rome. The *Digest* speaks of it as common. A number of plays of Plautus (late third to early second century BC) include the use of *arra*. And the same deposits show up again in actual contracts from the first-century AD archives from Pompeii. But in many of these transactions, both real and fictional, the so-called *arra* is also called a "pledge," is an item rather than a sum of money, and is occasionally part of a deal other than a sale. For instance, a loan is backed up with a store of grain [9]. A pledge (Chapter

12) is a separate institution native to Roman law. It is a form of contract in which a piece of property is offered as security for some other kind of payment, whether that payment is part of a sale, a lease, or a loan. On the one hand, the Romans seem to be taking a foreign institution and making it conform, more or less, to Roman rules. On the other hand, from a strictly Roman point of view, they could have just skipped the *arra* altogether and spoken only of pledges, at least in many cases. The fact that the Greek name is used anyway suggests that the very word had some point. In particular, it suggests a legal force for the term. A deposit or earnest money has practical and perhaps social effects even in a system where it has no special legal status, but it would have had those effects in Rome even if it were just called a pledge. It is worth adding the Greek name only if that name itself is thought to explain something new about the transaction. Here, then, we have an alien legal institution that had no official standing in the jurists' works and that was considerably reshaped by its contact with Roman law, but that still had at least a minor effect on the day-to-day workings of Roman law.

The last case is centered not on a particular legal institution but on a person. Some decades ago, we were lucky enough to recover from a cave in Israel the preserved remains of a set of second-century legal papers of a woman named Babatha. Most of these documents involve disputes over family property, though a few outside commercial transactions are included. The area had recently come under Roman rule, but the parties (mostly Jews) were not Roman citizens. There is tremendous debate over most of the specifics, but in general we can say that the disputes involved some combination of Roman law, internationalized Greek law, and some more local systems (Jewish and/or Nabataean Arab). It is difficult to figure out the precise balance in part because we have incomplete knowledge of all these systems and in part because the documents almost never make it clear what framework(s) they take for granted. Still, at a minimum we can say that at least some of the disputes were under the jurisdiction of Roman authorities. At least one of the disputes seems to have been framed not only by Roman formulary procedure (where a government official instructs [perhaps local] judges who actually decide the case), but also using the specific wording of a relevant Roman formula (Chapter 11; for the documents, see [26]). Several of the contracts end with a record of the question-and-answer ritual of the Roman *stipulatio* contract (Chapter 12). Now, it is possible that the Romanization here is quite shallow. Given the lack of supervision in the Roman judicial system even in Rome, a non-Roman judge, with or without benefit of a formula, might well rely on the substance of local laws. And the tacked-on references to *stipulatio* form suggest an audience that didn't really care (and perhaps didn't even really understand) what it was about. Still, some level of Romanization is undeniable. On the other hand, substantial elements of local law are still in play. Several of the documents revolve around the guardians of Babatha's son Jesus. Both the number of these and their method of appointment are non-Roman. Intestate succession in the documents seems to put sons ahead of daughters (contrary to Roman law;

see Chapter 15). And Babatha herself seems (though this is not entirely clear) to have been involved in a polygamous marriage. As in the reverse case, the "remnants" of local law may be quite shallow. In fact, it is not inconceivable that strictly Roman law was ultimately imposed on the persons named in the archive, despite the fact that they were trying to operate on more traditional principles. Nonetheless, it seems hard to doubt that the law governing this particular place at this particular time was "some of this and some of that," and probably more than a little of both.

22. CONCLUSION

❖❖❖❖❖❖❖❖❖

I BEGAN THIS BOOK with one Roman's mixed feelings about the law. For him, Roman law was both one of the great and distinctive accomplishments of human civilization and a some-what trivial game played by geeks for (at best) their own enter-tainment or (at worst) the legitimization of all kinds of mischief and even theft. The contexts in which Cicero was speaking suggest that both of his prejudices were widely held, at least in the elite circles in which he moved. He doesn't, that is, tell us about all Romans. In a sense, moreover, the texts I quoted there are largely theoretical. That is, one of them is entirely detached from any individual transaction or legal proceeding, and the other comes up only incidentally in the course of a trial on an unrelated matter. I want to conclude the book by briefly looking at the possibility of a similarly divided opinion of the law at more ordinary levels of society and in the heat of actual legal business.

The text I use to raise these questions for the sake of argu-ment is a fairly simple contract, somewhat remarkably pre-served, from the Netherlands ([25]). The underlying transaction is clear enough; one Stellus Reperius Boesus has sold a cow for

cash to another man named Gargilius Secundus in front of witnesses. The striking thing for present purposes is the final formula before the date at the end. "Let this agreement be free
from civil law (*ius civile*)." This is an odd thing to say in what
was presumably thought of by the writer as a "legal" document. Not only is the transaction a standard legal one (a sale;
see Chapter 12), but the text also speaks of "proper form" and
cites witnesses. (Arguments could be made against the ultimate
enforceability of this document, but the *parties* presumably
believed in it at the time.) Now, one explanation that might be
offered (and in fact has been offered) for the curious sentence is
a fairly technical one. The phrase actually appears elsewhere in
the Roman world in a context in which it is more appropriate.
It is sometimes found on tombs, which, as sacred things, are
not subject to ordinary commercial law (Chapter 20). They are
free from the "civil law" or *ius civile*, not in its broadest sense
of "the law of Rome," but in the narrower sense of "the law of
citizens" (as opposed to that of, say, the gods). It is possible,
then, that the writer of the contract knew "let this ... be free
from civil law" as an important legal formula without really
understanding it. After all, literate persons might easily see the
phrase often enough in public (on tombs) to recognize it, without ever having enough context to grasp its real meaning. We
can see the same kind of (faulty) diffusion of legal language in
our own society. The legal term of art "malice aforethought"
applies strictly only to homicide (and does not have much to
do with "malice" or "forethought" in their ordinary senses),
but in folk usage is applied to a variety of crimes and in a sense

relying on the word-by-word interpretation. An even closer parallel might be provided by a phenomenon I have noticed in my own experience as a member of the board of directors of a condominium residence. The board from time to time receives letters of complaint about its actions or policies. The writers are aware that they are entering into a relatively formal realm, and one with potential legal consequences. Hence they tend to include as much "legal" language as they can — phrases like "breaking and entering," "retain counsel," "cease and desist" — even if those phrases are not strictly applicable. In fact, in the jurisdiction where I live, the phrase "breaking and entering" is not technically part of the law at all any more.

More generally, we are familiar with a whole range of folk legal knowledge in our own society — bits of real, mistaken, and simply imaginary legal information passed on by a variety of sources. News coverage and courtroom dramas are often correct, if oversimplified or incomplete. Other sources, like political speeches and even comedians' jokes, are less reliable, but still help to shape folk law. For instance, most viewers of American police dramas know at least roughly the wording of the *Miranda* warning to criminal suspects ("You have the right to remain silent...") and the reasons for its use. Further from real law is the commonly held belief that individual students are prohibited from engaging in prayer in American public schools. (Only school-sponsored religious activity raises constitutional issues.) Less seriously, comedians often joke about the supposedly real (if rarely applied) penalties for removing mattress tags. Of course, as even the tags themselves make clear, this penalty applies only to dealers, not to the end user. Still, the legal "knowledge" involved has a recognizable source in a genuine legal document. In Rome, a character in a comedy of the mid second century BC jokes that he doesn't care whether he gets hold of a woman he desires "by stealth, force, or permission," playing on the phrase from the interdicts (Chapter 13). And several centuries later, someone took the trouble to inscribe what look to be the rules of a drinking game in the official form used for statutes passed by the assembly. The language of the law filtered down to the Romans, too. So perhaps the writer who tried to shoo away the civil law was actually, in a clumsy way, trying to harness its power.

But perhaps there is a deeper issue at stake, and perhaps the writer of the contract was more seriously conflicted. "Let this agreement be free from civil law" could be interpreted as a genuine attempt to opt out of some or all of the legal system. In the former case, the idea would be to avoid appeal to legal institutions, that is, a trial and the related proceedings. Thus it might be like the clauses in most American credit card and cell phone contracts that move disputes from the (public) courts to (private) arbitration (paid for, not incidentally, by the industries in question). Or consider how the possibility of no-fault divorce encourages spouses to negotiate a settlement on their own, which is only ratified after the fact by a judge. The latter case would mean a move outside of the legal system entirely. While cash sale is one of the situations Roman law is comfortable with handling, it certainly exists without that law, and the Romans knew this. In fact, the general notion of voluntary exchange of goods clearly exists as a social institution outside of any legal system at all. The parties to this "contract" might then be saying that their agreement wasn't really a "contract" after all; they didn't want their "gentleman's agreement" to be co-opted by the legal system and so taken at least partially out of their control.

Why opt out of the legal system in either of these senses? There are at least a couple of reasons. As mentioned in the introduction, law (like rhetoric) was a package of specialized knowledge available only to the few. This might not have bothered a Cicero, but it could be a concern for our Boesus and Secundus. But there is also a problem that might have bothered everyone. Whatever its gaps and flaws, Roman law became a relatively large and independent system. It was not entirely under the control of any individual, perhaps not even under the emperors', and certainly not that of ordinary lawyers and litigants. The law might give the "wrong" decision because a particular case raised issues that had not previously been factored in. Or, as we have seen throughout this book, there are many circumstances in which there is no clear "right" answer, and the law must make somewhat arbitrary choices about what values to preserve, about who will lose out when someone has to take the fall. The losing parties in these cases are likely to take a short-term view and claim that the law got it "wrong." Turning law into a system opens up a space between it and "justice," or at least so it can be made to seem.

I must admit that it is not clear that any of this is going on in our document. An arbitration clause, if that is what was intended, would probably have been written in more positive terms. Total rejection of the law would perhaps make more sense as a sentiment expressed orally by the parties, rather than quickly written into the contract. Still, it is hard not to see some nervousness in the parties to this deal. On the one hand, they use a legal mechanism to exchange livestock for money, and our knowledge of the law of sale can tell us a lot about the consequences of that choice. At the same time, their faith in that mechanism is clearly not total. We can also see this in a plaque labeling a tomb access road that says "Let trickery (*dolus malus*) and civil law (*ius civile*) be away from all these." This usage is superficially closer to the "correct" one, since a tomb is at least nearby. Yet the text really refers to the road rather than to the tomb. And the connection made between the civil law and trickery is ironic, since *dolus* is itself a legal term of art. So here too the writer seems to be trying to use the power of legal language to fend off the evils lurking within the legal system. The legal world of *these* Romans (starting with the question of what kind of "Romans" they were) was a complicated one.

DOCUMENTS

⟨⟨⟨⟨⟨⟨⟨⟨

WHERE ARE THESE DOCUMENTS FROM?

The bulk of the documents presented here come from a single source, and so they can provide a certain amount of context for each other. They are written on a series of wax-covered tablets excavated at Muricine near ancient Pompeii (itself near modern Naples, but buried by a volcanic eruption in AD 79). Most of them involve the business affairs of a family called the Sulpicii. This gives them their (Latin) name, "Tabulae Pompeianae Sulpiciorum," and the abbreviation commonly used to identify them – TPSulp. They date from the early to mid first century AD (as you will see, many of the individual documents give dates, sometimes including the year).

The other texts (following those from TPSulp) come from a wide variety of times and places and are recorded in various media: more wax tablets, inscribed marble, inscribed bronze, papyrus. Most of these are identified here by the numbers given them in a standard collection of Roman legal documents (S. Riccobono, *Fontes Iuris Romani Anteiustiniani* [Florence, 1940–3]). The last three come from miscellaneous other sources.

All but [26] and parts of [14, 17] (in Greek) were originally written in Latin.

A NOTE ON NAMES

Male Roman citizens had three names, and they normally used all three in formal, legal contexts, like "Gaius Sulpicius Faustus" and "Lucius Faenius Eumenes" in the first document. The middle of the three is a clan name, shared by (among others) people with a shared male ancestor, as well as by the former slaves of that family (who, as ex-slaves, are themselves citizens; see Chapter 10). In these texts, the third name is the most distinctive and is often used to identify individuals. Women typically have two names, one of which is the feminine form of their clan name. (So the sisters of the men just named would have "Sulpicia" and "Faenia" in their names, respectively.)

Non-Romans typically have a single name. Free aliens of either sex are identified by the combination of their own name, their father's name, and their city of origin, like "Zenon of Tyre" in the second text. Slaves are identified by their own name and that of their owner.

Ex-slaves, of whatever nationality, are often identified by their former owner's name, though we can't really tell if that is always the case.

Most names in the documents ending in -us, -os, or -es belong to men; those ending in -a (except Arpocra in [4]) or in -is are women's.

[1] TPSulp 2

Guarantee-of-appearance made by Gaius Sulpicius Faustus for next 24 June in the Forum of Puteoli in front of the Hordonian altar of Augustus at 9 AM. As part of an action in the matter of a sale, Lucius Faenius Eumenes asked for a formal promise for HS[1] 50,000; Gaius Sulpicius Faustus made the promise. Done at Puteoli.

- Eumenes is suing Faustus over a sale. This tablet records a *vadimonium* (a promise of bond or bail) guaranteeing Faustus's appearance at a hearing in this matter. There are other documents in the archive recording their ongoing legal struggles.
- This guarantee is achieved by means of the contract form called *stipulatio*, illustrated by the question-and-answer recorded in this document. *Stipulatio* could be used for any purpose, since it was defined by that form, not by its substance. Technically, the *stipulatio* was an oral contract, so this document is a record or would-be evidence, but we probably should not say that it "is" the contract.

[2] TPSulp 4

Guarantee-of-appearance made by Zenon of Tyre, freedman of Zenobius, for the coming 11 June in the Forum of Puteoli

---

[1] "HS" is the Roman abbreviation for a standard unit of currency, the *"sesterce."*

in front of the Hordonian altar of Augustus at 9 AM. Gaius Sulpicius Cinnamus asked that HS 1200 be promised, and Zenon of Tyre, freedman of Zenobius, made the promise. Done at Puteoli 9 June 52.

- This *vadimonium* has the same function as the previous document. In this case, however, we see that the promiser is a non-Roman, and so not technically eligible to make a *stipulatio*. As a result, slightly different words are used in Latin for "promise," and this is not technically a *stipulatio* (thought the practical effect seems to have been the same – as also in [10]).
- Roman law made freed slaves of Romans into Roman citizens. Here a freedman of a Tyrian is treated as a Tyrian himself. This probably reflects the creeping use of Roman legal principles abroad rather than a careful investigation of Tyrian law.

[3] TPSulp 23

An inheritance hearing before Lucius Granius Probus, *duumvir*.[2] Gaius Sulpicius Faustus asked Aulus Castricius Onesimus whether he was heir to Aulus Castricius Isochrysus and in what share. Aulus Castricius Onesimus replied that he was heir to Aulus Castricius Isochrysus with a 1/12 plus a fifth of a 1/24

---

[2] "*Duumvir*" (something like a modern "mayor," but literally just "one of two guys") was the title given to the chief magistrates of many Roman towns, much as the two consuls were the chief executives of the central government.

share (= 11/120) 28 April 35. [Names of witnesses who applied their seals to the document follow.]

- Roman wills focused not on distribution of individual items but rather on passing on the estate (assets and liabilities alike) as a whole. Thus, if there are to be multiple beneficiaries, they often get small, elaborately calculated fractions like these. A separate document suggests that the will may have been partially overturned in favor of the patron of Isochrysus (such partial action was possible only in very limited circumstances). The object of the suit documented here seems to have been to recover Isochrysus's debts from his heirs.
- This hearing was held before a local elected official (*in iure*), serving much the same role at Pompeii as the praetor in Rome, rather than before a judge (*apud iudicem*). This kind of hearing served to establish the basic outlines of the case, but there would not be a formal airing of the evidence, confrontation, or judgment until the hearing before the judge.

[4] TPSulp 43

Titus Vestorius Arpocra the younger asked for a promise that ... [the slave] was not a fugitive and wanderer and that the other things required in this year's edict of the curule aediles had been correctly provided for and that the conventional double-price-back guarantee was in place. Titus Vestorius Phoenix made the promise. Done at Puteoli 21 August 38. [Witnesses.]

- While the urban praetor's Edict was the most important source of law, other magistrates could issue edicts, and that of the aediles was important for certain commercial guarantees, including (as here) guarantees that must be offered on sales of slaves. The aediles' authority was originally over the markets at Rome, but this document suggests that it was eventually generalized.

- We happen to know that some jurists insisted that a guarantee of the form *"that* a slave was not a runaway" or the like was invalid, and that instead a penalty should be guaranteed in case it turned out that the condition was true. This contract seems to do both. It may also confuse the required guarantee of compensation for defects (ill health, runaway or wanderer, attached legal liabilities) with the double-value guarantee if the original seller turned out not to be the real owner.

[5] TPSulp 45

Written-commitment of Diognetus, slave of Gaius Novius Cypaerus, for the lease of bin 12 in the Bassian granaries, in which is grain received from Gaius Novius Eunus as a pledge. 2 July 37. I, Diognetus, slave of Gaius Novius Cypaerus, have written at the order of my master, Cypaerus, in his presence that I [on the "I," see notes] have leased to Hesicus, slave of Aevenius, freedman of Tiberius Iulius Augustus, bin 12 in the middle of the Bassian public granaries of Puteoli, in which is placed Alexandrian grain which he received today from Gaius

Novius Eunus as a pledge. Also the spaces between the columns in the lower level of the same granary, where he has 200 sacks of legumes, which he has received as a pledge from the same Eunus. Month-to-month from 1 July, at a rate of HS 1. Done at Puteoli.

- This document records two contracts: primarily a lease (of storage space) but also a pledge (cf. [8]) to a third party (of the grain stored there). This is not unlike modern rental agreements, where the goods stored serve as security for payments on the storage space. (It is likely, but not explicit, that the pledge is tied to the lease.)
- Roman law requires a cash price to make a valid lease, but the amount here is purely nominal (imagine renting a space for a dollar or a pound per month). This suggests that the two sides have a more complicated business relationship than the rental represented here. Eunus and Cypaerus are probably business partners, or even freedman and patron.
- Here Cypaerus is represented by his slave Diognetus. Since Roman law did not like to create business agents, and since slaves could not own or acquire on their own behalf, they could be used to extend the reach of their owners, allowing them to do business without showing up in person. The text clearly reads "I leased," but some feel that this is a (mistaken) direct quotation, and that Cypaerus actually did the leasing. If so, then the same error also occurs in the next document.

[6] TPSulp 46

Written-commitment of Nardus, slave of Publius Annius Seleucus, for the lease of bin 26 ... for Publius Annius Seleucus 13 March 40. I, Nardus, slave of Publius Annius Seleucus, have written in the presence and by the order of my master, Publius Annius Seleucus, because he says he does not know his letters, that I have leased to Gaius Sulpicius Faustus bin 26, which is in the upper Barbatian properties of Domitia Lepida in which lie 13,000 *modii*[3] of Alexandrian wheat, which my master along with his slaves have measured out. Month-to-month at a rate of HS 100. Done at Puteoli. [Witnesses.]

- The underlying transaction here is largely the same as in the previous document, but the rental rate is higher. Unfortunately, we don't really know if this is the market price, or still involves a discount for people in business together.
- Here the slave writes the document, despite the fact that the owner is explicitly said to be present. Here the slave is more literate, probably not an uncommon situation, so that may be the actual reason for the slave's writing [5]. We will also see a third possible reason in [16].
- Another document (not shown here) suggests that the grain is security for a cash loan.

---

[3] A *modius* was a unit of measurement, somewhat larger than the gallon.

[7] TPSulp 48

I, Gaius Iulius Prudens, have written that I asked Gaius
Sulpicius Cinnamus and entrusted him with the task of [paying
out so much money] as he or Eros or [name missing] or Titianus
or Martialis [his slaves] or Gaius Sulpicius Faustus or anyone
else at the order request or commission of any of them gave,
entrusted, promised, or offered security for, or assumed the
risk for in any way to Suavis my freedman or Hyginus my slave
or anyone else at their order. Gaius Sulpicius Cinnamus asked
for a promise that as much be given [to him] as money was so
given, entrusted, or assumed the obligation for in any way (as
was listed above), and that there be no fraud attached to this
promise now or in the future on my part or that of my heir and
anyone else to whom this matter pertains, and that if there is
fraud, its value be paid to him, and that these things be duly
done and paid, and I, Gaius Iulius Prudens, promised.

- The crucial phrase "paying ... money" near the beginning
  is not actually in the text. Some such words were apparently
  left out and have to be guessed at. It is not clear whether this
  is a mere "typo" in the copying of a longish text or whether
  it represents a deeper problem with the drafting of such a
  complicated document.
- The "entrusting" at the beginning is not a mere request for a
  favor, but a kind of contract. The party extracting the favor
  was legally responsible for paying the costs of having the
  favor carried out.

- The general idea is to consolidate all the business affairs between Prudens and his associates and Cinnamus and his associates into a single set of obligations of Prudens to Cinnamus. Parts of this (especially having to do with the slaves) seem redundant, and other parts perhaps would not take effect quickly enough. There is debate among scholars today about whether this represents poor legal work by the parties, or whether it just illustrates their extra caution. The clear gap in the text makes it even harder than usual to resolve this kind of question.

- The clause at the end about fraud is a standard provision.

[8] TPSulp 49

11 January 49. I, Purgias, son of Alexander, have written that I made a request of Gaius Sulpicius Cinnamus and entrusted to him that he make over ... African and Italian ... to Trophimus, *vicarius* of Cerinthus, slave of the emperor, as security, at the rate of HS 1 per HS 125,000....

- The "security" mentioned in this passage involved transferring the actual ownership of collateral to the creditor, then recovering it later, after the debt had been paid. The form of security in most of these documents (see above on "pledge") instead gave the creditor the right to collect in the future, in case of default. Pledge seems to have been a more "modern" development, but it apparently did not drive out the older form entirely.

- A *"vicarius"* is a slave "owned" (technically, in the *peculium* of) another slave. See Chapter 10.

[9] TPSulp 51

Written-commitment of Gaius Novius Eunus for a loan of HS 10,000 at Puteoli 18 June 37. I, Gaius Novius Eunus, have written that I have accepted HS 10,000 in cash as a loan from Evenus Primianus (who was not present), freedman of Tiberius Caesar Augustus, by way of Hesychus his slave, and I owe to him this sum, which I will return to him when he requests it. Hesychus, slave of Evenus Primianus, freedman of Tiberius Caesar Augustus, asked for a formal promise for the above-specified HS 10,000; I, Gaius Novius Eunus, made the promise. For these HS 10,000 in cash I gave him roughly 7000 *modii* of Alexandrian grain as pledge and *arrabo* and roughly 4,000 *modii* of chickpeas, spelt, and lentils in 200 sacks, all of which I have stored in my area at the Bassian public granary at Puteoli, which I admit is at my own risk from all danger. Done at Puteoli.

- Here we have a loan. That transaction is protected by a "real" contract on its own, but here we have the form of a *stipulatio* used.
- Here a slave explicitly participates to extend the owner's reach (cf. [5, 6])
- What this document calls *"arrabo"* seems to be a fairly normal pledge of the type seen in [2]. It is perhaps striking,

then, that Eunus chose to describe it by a foreign name, especially since it seems to fit the Roman rules better than the foreign (Chapter 21).

- An additional clause at the end of the agreement puts the risks of damage to the grain on Eunus, who has offered it as security, but retained physical possession. This arrangement would have been in effect anyway (the creditor was responsible only for security in his possession, and then not against all dangers), but it at least provides clarity.

[10] TPSulp 54

Written-commitment of Marcus Lollius Philippus for HS 20,000. Written-commitment of Gaius Avilius Cinnamus on behalf of Marcus Lollius Philippus 3 October 45. I, Marcus Lollius Philippus, have written that I received HS 20,000 in cash as a loan and owe it to Gaius Sulpicius Cinnamus. Gaius Sulpicius Cinnamus asked for a formal promise for the above-specified HS 20,000; I, Marcus Lollius Philippus, made the promise. Done at Puteoli 3 October of the same date. I, Gaius Avilius Cinnamus, have written at the prompting of Gaius Sulpicius Cinnamus that I have made a guarantee for the above-specified HS 20,000 at my own risk on behalf of Marcus Lollius Philippus and Gaius Sulpicius Cinnamus. Moreover, I declare have sworn by Jupiter and by the guardian spirit of the divine Augustus that I have not served as guarantee for the same men in any other matter this year. Done at Puteoli.

- Several of the documents above referred to real security — that is, cash or items that would back up payment, as we are familiar with today. Roman law was also very interested in "personal security." This is like a person "cosigning" for a modern loan, guaranteeing payment if the primary borrower does not make good.

- The underlying debt is created by a loan (a real contract; see Chapter 12), so this transaction is protected by two contracts. Interestingly, neither explicitly mentions an interest rate.

- The oath does not have a specific legal force here (cf. [12]). Oaths could bring an end to a case, but only if both sides agreed in advance (a procedure that does seem to be reflected elsewhere in this archive).

- The limit on multiple guarantees in the last sentence was required by law, though the phrasing here may be slightly wrong.

[11] TPSulp 56

Written-commitment of Niceros, slave of the colonists, for HS 1,000 for next 1 July 52. 7 March 52. I, Niceros, slave treasurer of the colonists of Puteoli, have written that I have received HS 1,000 in cash as a loan and owe them to Gaius Sulpicius Cinnamus. Gaius Sulpicius Cinnamus asked for a formal promise for the above-specified HS 1,000 to be paid next 1 July; I, Niceros, slave treasurer of the colonists of Puteoli, made the promise. HS 1,000 for next 1 July.

• Here we have a receipt for money loaned (as in [9]), but the borrower is the city of Puteoli. The city is represented in this transaction not as a corporation, but by the person of the treasurer (it happens that I write my property-tax checks to one "Nelda Wells-Spears" (the county tax collector—assessor) rather than to "Travis County"). The use of a public (i.e., city-owned) slave here, rather than an elected magistrate, clarifies the situation, since the former could be transacting only on behalf of his owner, while the latter might be working for himself.

[12] TPSulp 60

Accounts of Titinia Antracis

Paid out to Euplia of Melos, daughter of Theodorus, with the approval of her tutor Epichares of Athens, son of Alexander: HS 1,600. He asked for and received HS 1,600 from her domestic chest...

For the chest. Epichares of Athens, son of Aphrodisius, at the prompting of Titinia Antracis, offered a guarantee to Titinia Antracis for the above-mentioned HS 1,600 in cash on behalf of Eulpia of Melos, daughter of Theodorus. Done at Puteoli 20 March 43.

• On the one hand, this document is formally different from most of the above because it is a record for the creditor's own accounting of what happened, not the agreement of the loan itself. On the other hand, even those "contracts" were technically just evidence of agreements that were created orally, by hand-over, or by the mere fact of agreement, so in practice a record like this might serve the same function.

• The debtor, Euplia, needs the approval of her tutor because she is contracting an obligation. Since she is not a Roman citizen, it is not clear that the whole apparatus of guardianship actually applied to her, but it may have seemed safer or just customary. Moreover, this extension of Roman practice may have been encouraged by the fact that many other legal systems of the day had at least roughly similar notions of guardianship of women. Titinia did not need any approval, since she did not acquire any new obligations.

[13] TPSulp 68

15 September 39. I, Gaius Novius Eunus, have written that I owe HS 1,250 in cash to Hesycus Euenianus, slave of Gaius Caesar Augustus Germanicus, left after all accounts have been calculated, which I received from him as a loan and which sum I promised on oath to Jupiter Best and Greatest and the guardian spirits of the late Augustus and of Gaius Caesar Augustus that I would return either to Hesychus himself or to Gaius Sulpicius Faustus next 1 November, and if I do not pay up on this day, I will not only be guilty of perjury, but I will be obliged in the amount of HS 20 per day as a penalty. Hesychus, slave of Gaius Caesar, asked for a formal promise for the above-mentioned

HS 1,250; I, Gaius Novius Eunus, made that promise. Done at Puteoli.

- It appears from the first sentence and other documents that Eunus and Hesycus have an ongoing business relationship (cf. [5]), and that the main point of the present contract is to bring all the obligations in both directions under a single accounting. There are other similar examples in the archive.
- The next-to-last sentence gives an example of a term added by the parties even though it was not required to complete the contract. If the loan is not paid by the specified date, then the debtor will be liable for a further daily penalty (which would amount to an almost 600% rate of interest from that point).

[14] TPSulp 78

I, Quintus Aelius Romanus, have written at the request and order of Marcus Barbatus Celer in his presence (because he says he does not know his letters) that he made a guarantee for the above-mentioned 1,000 *denarii*[4] to Primus, slave of Publius Attius Severus, on behalf of Menelaus of Ceramos, son of Irenaeus, as is written above.

- Here we have another document written for the benefit of an illiterate (cf. [6]). Somewhat unusually, the writer is a Roman citizen himself, and not (apparently) a dependent. The text

---

[4] A *"denarius"* is another unit of currency, equivalent to four *sesterces*.

comes paired with a Greek version that indicates that the underlying contract is for naval transport.

[15] TPSulp 79

15 March 40. I, Lucius Marius Iucundus, freedman of Dida, wrote that I gave 13,000 *modii* of Alexandrian grain to Gaius Sulpicius Faustus, grain which rests in bin 26 of the upper Barbatian granary of Domitia Lepida as a pledge against HS 20,000, which I have written in a document I owe to him. If next 15 May I have not repaid the above-mentioned HS 20,000 or arranged security, then you will be permitted to sell at auction the grain in question under the condition of the pledge in question. If you sell it for more, return the difference to me; if for less, I will return the difference to you or your heir. We have discussed and I have agreed that the grain in question is at my risk or that of my heir. Done at Puteoli.

- Here is a pledge to back up a loan (as in [9]), but in this case the loan may have existed well before the pledge. At the very least we would expect some clearer record of its terms in another document.
- This contains the most elaborate extra clauses of any of the documents here. There is the possibility of selling the pledges (which can be avoided by payment or by giving alternative security). If the sale goes ahead, then the money will be distributed differently, depending on whether the underlying debt is covered. Additionally, we have a clause specifying where the risk lies.

[16] TPSulp 82

5 December 43. I, Lucius Patulcius Epaphroditus, have written at the request and command of my freedwoman Patulcia Erotis in her presence that she received from Gaius Sulpicius Cinnamus HS 19,500 in cash from his auction. On the basis of the sealed tablets. Done at Puteoli.

- Here a freedman writes for his patroness, and it is possible that this is just another example of writing for a less literate owner/patron, and perhaps even evidence for a lower level of literacy among women than men. On the other hand, there is no explicit mention of her (il)literacy. This happens often enough that some have argued that there was a social taboo on women writing legal documents, even if they had the skill to do so.
- The mention of the sealed tablets (which neither proves nor is proven by anything here) might support the theory that their form seemed especially authoritative to the Romans.
- Many of the documents in this archive refer to auction sales. These seem to have been common in the Roman world, but we do not know of any special legal provisions they generated.

[17] FIRA 3.24

To Claudius Valerius Firmus, praefect of Egypt from Aurelia Ammonaria. Sir, I ask that you give me Aurelius Plutamnon as tutor in accordance with the *lex Iulia et Titia* and decrees of the Senate. Given AD 247.

I, Aurelia Ammonaria, have submitted this.

I, Aurelius Plutamnon, concur in this petition.

So long as your proper guardian not be removed from guardianship, I give you Plutammon as tutor in accordance with the *lex Iulia et Titia* and decrees of the Senate.

- Since the governor's response is conditional, he can issue an order directly in response to the petition, without holding a fact-finding hearing first (cf. the use of interdicts, discussed in Chapter 13).
- The law mentioned at the end dated from the mid first century BC and gave governors the authority to make these appointments within their provinces.
- Here we have a single document written by several persons and even in multiple languages. The first and last parts (the formal petition, perhaps written by a professional scribe, and the governor's response) are in Latin; the second and third (personal affirmations) are in Greek.

[18] FIRA 3.47

Antonius Silvanus, cavalryman of the first Mauritanean troop of Thracians, assistant to the prefect, squad of Valerius, made this will. Let Marcus Antonius Satrianus, my son, be sole heir of all my goods, both in camp and at home; all others are hereby disinherited. Let him accept my estate within 100 days. If he does not do so, let him be disinherited. Then in the second case, let my brother ... Antonius be my heir, and let him accept my estate in the next 60 days. If he is not my heir, I give him as a legacy 750 *denarii*. I name as curator of my goods in camp, for their collection and restoration to Antonia Thermutha, mother of my heir, Hierax, son of Behax, elite soldier of the same troop, the squad of Aebutius, so that she may guard it herself until my son and heir comes into his own and receives it from her. I give Hierax 500 *denarii* as a legacy. I give Antonia Thermutha, mother of my heir, 500 *denarii* as a legacy. I give my prefect 500 *denarii* as a legacy. As for my slave Cronio, I wish him to be free after my death so long as he handles everything correctly and hands it over to my heir or procurator, and that the manumission tax be paid out of my estate. Let fraud be absent from this will. [A list of witnesses, some of whom participated in the ritual, follows.]

- This illustrates the two different ways to leave property in a will. Here four people are given fixed "legacies"; Satrianus (or, if he does not accept, Antonius) is "heir" to the rest of the remaining assets and liabilities of the estate, and in fact is correctly described as the "sole heir," even though others profit from the will.

- The clause "all others are hereby disinherited" is designed to protect the will in case Antonius had (or could be claimed to have) other direct descendants besides his son. They would have to be made co-heirs or (as here) explicitly disinherited.

- Silvanus was an active-duty soldier and so was not allowed to be married at this time (AD 142). Hence his son could not have been legitimate, so it was necessary to make him heir by will, since he would not inherit by intestate succession (Chapter 15).

[19] FIRA 3.54

I, the honorable Postumius Iulianus, of sound body and mind, mindful of human mortality, have made this will.... Out of my Praenestine parcel I wish that the house which is called Fulgerita in the territory of Praeneste in the region of Campania be given to all the citizens of Praeneste, so that they may honor my spirit annually in memory of me, and set up a statue in my name in the Forum and inscribe the text of this testament on it, and no one is to have the power of removing it, and if there is an attempt to alienate it, the public treasury is to take possession.

- Like many modern wills, this one contains instructions in addition to simple distributions of property. This is an excerpt from the full will, so it does not include the institution of an heir or other required technicalities.
- It turns out the Cicero passage mocking how lawyers named pieces of land (Chapter 1) was not so far wrong (though perhaps still unfair).

[20] FIRA 3.64

In the matter between, on the one hand, Dionysius, son of Manlius, cavalryman (ret.), whom Marcus Trebius Heraclides, horseman of the Aprian troop, squad of Acamans, son of this Dionysius, and, on the other, Marcus Apronius and Marcus Manlius, horsemen of the troop of the Vocontii, squad of Domesticus, about degree of relationship, that is, which of them is closer to Dionysius, son of Manlius, horseman of the Aprian troop, for purposes of taking possession of his estate, since he is said to have died intestate, L. Silius Laetus, prefect of the camp, designated P. Matius of Legion III Cyrenaica as judge and ordered him to pass judgment.

Publius Matius of Legion III Cyrenaica, after he summoned [several decurions of other troops] to assist and both sides pleaded their cases and their affidavits were read, spoke his verdict: it seemed to him that Dionysius, son of Manlius, was the brother of the brother of the deceased Dionysius, but that Apronius and Manlius are sons of the sister of this Dionysius, who produced documents of the relationship, and the goods in question of Dionysius were to be adjudged to this Dionysius, son of Manlius, cavalryman (ret.).

Done in Egypt in Camp [name lost], in the Heliopolite *nome*,[5] November 42 [the precise date is uncertain].

- This is an extremely rare example of a decision rendered in a particular case that was actually litigated. Unlike many

---

[5] *"Nomes"* were local administrative districts peculiar to Egypt.

modern judicial decisions, it gives no hint of the grounds on which it was made.

- The citizenship of the deceased and his heir is uncertain, nor do we know whether the case was decided on the basis of Roman or local law. (If the people were not Romans, then even the application of "normal" Roman law would be a special adaptation to local conditions; inheritance normally followed the personality principle.)

[21] FIRA 3.80s

[Name missing] made this for himself and his most upright wife, Arecusa, and his freedmen and freedwomen and their descendants and the freedmen of Arescusa. This monument does not go to the heir.

- Family tombs, such as this, were common in Rome, but the definition of "family" was ambiguous. The law recognized one type of tomb that was available to the *familia*, that is, the entire household, apparently what is intended here. There is another that goes to the heirs of the deceased for their own later use. In strict law, freedpersons were not entitled to co-burial unless they were heirs, but the rule seems to have been widely ignored, as even our legal sources admit. The final phrase excluding the heirs is abbreviated, just using the first letter of each word in Latin, showing how common the expression was.
- The inclusion of freedmen is also very common in tomb inscriptions, though some jurists questioned the validity of

such clauses in cases where they were not already qualified to be buried.

[22] FIRA 3.81g+h

May these gardens serve my ashes free from servitude obligations, for I will guarantee succession of guardians always to feast from the income of these gardens on my birthday and bring roses. I wish these gardens not be divided or alienated.

To the gods of the dead. Marcus Ulpius Symphorus, freedman of the emperor, maker of gold and silver coins [made this] for himself and Ulpia Helpidis, his freedwoman and wife, and for Ulpia, daughter of Arsinoe and Claudius Anthiocianus, son of his freedwoman Helpidis, and the freedpeople of my house of either sex to hold their remains and for such descendants as retain my name, on the condition that they not mortgage this tomb (or "monument") nor sell it and that there be no other way for anyone to alienate it. This monument does not go to the heir.

- The waffling between "monument" and "tomb" (cf. the next text and [23c]) seems to be a defense against lawyers who might take advantage of the fact that it was the latter word that triggered all the special rules about sacred land. "Monument" is, in Latin as in English, a more general word, but in normal usage both languages would allow the same structure to be called both things).

• Both of these inscriptions offer restrictions on the sale of the tomb. It appears that these should be redundant (since sacred land in general cannot be sold), but such restrictions are so common that many have suspected that we are missing some important technicality.

[23] FIRA 3.85c+f

[Person's name lost from inscription] requested from the pontiffs that they permit him to restore this monument on his own authority for his freedmen and women and himself and the descendants of these.

The aediles give permission that a body be placed in this monument (or "tomb").

• The pontiffs were the "priests" charged with interpreting most of religious law, and especially that related to sacred land, so it is not surprising that they would be asked for permission in the first text. The intervention of secular authorities (the aediles) in the second text is perhaps more surprising.

• For the application of similar rules in the provinces, see [27].

[24] FIRA 3.106 a, c, f, i, and m

There is a right of passage on foot or driving into this shrine of Feronia from this grove on the (public) via Campana, at which point it is closest, for 1,210 feet.

The road is private from the public highway, through the garden, attached to the monument (or "tomb"), which Agathopus, freedman of Augustus, a herald, and Iunia Epictesis made while still alive. Let trickery and civil law be away from all these.

Private road of Annius Largus. Antonius Astralis uses it by permission.

The lower road is the private property of Titus Umbrenus, son of Gaius. Passage is by permission. Let no one lead a herd or plow.

Rights to pass on foot or driving to the well and drawing of water from the Rutilian aqueduct outside the city come with purchase of this.

- Servitudes could be claimed by appeal to past use and lost by disuse. Hence the need to have posted notices to claim their existence (a, c, m). It was also important to specify that passage over private property was "by permission" (f, i) so that habitual use did not give rise to a permanent servitude.

- The third and fourth texts mention particular individuals, but (as the fifth one illustrates), servitudes were actually tied to the land.

- Servitudes granted only rights broad enough to achieve their basic purpose, so when the first text specifies that the shortest route must be taken by those going from the main road to the grove, it is just spelling out something the law already implied.

[25] FIRA 3.137

I, Gargilius Secundus, have bought a cow from Stellus Reperius Beosus at the Villa of Lopeteus in proper form for HS 125. Cesdius, centurion of legion V, and Mutus Admetus, centurion of legion I Rapax, served as witnesses. Let this agreement be free from civil law. Bought on 9 September [date uncertain].

- A basic cash sale of a cow. For discussion of the final provision, see Chapter 22.
- The word translated above as "Rapax" (the nickname of a legion) is indicated by the abbreviation "R." There are other interpretations of this, including the idea that it stands for "*redhibitio*" (return of the item after sale) and that the last clause says no return will be allowed here.

[26] P. Yadin 28–30

Between A, son of B (plaintiff), and X, son of Y (defendant), up to a value of 2,500 *denarii*, let there be judges. Since X served as guardian of A (which is the matter at hand), when X should in good faith give something to or do something for A, let the judges award that up to a limit of 2,500 *denarii*. Otherwise, let them acquit.

- The archive of Babatha contained three apparently identical copies of this formula, written in Greek. It is virtually certain that this is the standard formula for the action to be used by a young person demanding that his or her former guardians account for their management of the property. But that does not appear to be the proper action to be used in any of the cases attested elsewhere in the archive. This has given rise to many theories and questions, but it is hard to answer any of them without assuming answers to the others.

- Who is the source of this Greek translation of what was presumably a Latin original? If it came from the governor and his staff, was it part of a general publication, or did they provide it to fit Babatha's situation, or did they provide it by specific request (without caring what it would be used for)?

- Did the vagueness of the formula allow it to be used in a broader variety of circumstances in the provinces? Was it meant for an unattested (and perhaps much later) action? Was it perhaps simply the wrong document to file altogether?

[27] Pliny, Letters 68 and 69

Pliny to Emperor Trajan

Since many have petitioned that, in accord with the example of (previous) governors, I permit them to transfer the remains of their family members on account of the ravages of age or flooding or other similar reasons, and since I know that in Rome application is normally made to the college of Pontiffs in such cases, I thought that I should ask you, my lord, the Chief Pontiff, what you would prefer I do.

Trajan to Pliny

It is harsh to impose on provincials the need to apply to the pontiffs, if they want to transfer the remains of their family members from one place to another for some just cause. Instead, you should follow the example of those previously in charge of your province and grant or deny permission as each individual case demands.

- How general is this ruling? Trajan refers to the practice of Pliny's predecessors in Bithynia, but does that mean he would give different general instructions to the governor of another province, or just that each governor should adopt the (varying) local practices? Does Trajan offer some respect for the substance of local religious practice? If so, a similar ruling might be made in many similar cases. Or does he just want to avoid the procedural problem of having provincials appeal to the pontiffs in Rome? If so, then this might be a very narrow ruling.
- Whatever the details, this decision seems to move practical authority from religious authorities to secular ones. This is less a matter of growing separation between church and state than of putting all authority in the hands of men who answer directly to the emperor, himself the chief pontiff.

GLOSSARY

Action. The term is used to describe both a particular proceeding ("The plaintiff in this action is Bob") and the form of remedy in a general legal circumstance ("The law gives an action on sale, but not on barter").

Aedile. One of the lesser magistrates (*see* below) in the Roman government who was in charge of (among other things) the markets. They produced an edict that contained some important regulations for commerce.

Agnate. Two persons descended through men from a shared male ancestor are called agnates. Roman law, especially in earlier times, tended to define families in terms of agnates.

Alienate. To give up ownership of property, whether by gift, sale, or otherwise.

Apud iudicem. "Before a judge." The second phase of a Roman trial under the formulary procedure, in which the parties argued the specific facts of the case and a decision was rendered.

Bonae fidei. "According to good faith." The standard by which cases involving (among other things) consensual contracts were decided. The judge was given considerable flexibility to account for business conventions, special circumstances, and the difference between large and small violations of agreements. Contrast *stricti iuris*.

Civil law. The family of legal systems descended (more or less directly) from Roman law. Most of the law of continental Europe is civil.

Common law. The legal system of Great Britain and its descendants (including the United States).

Consul. The highest ranking of the Roman magistrates (*see* below). Two served at a time, sharing (in theory) the powers of the former kings, though these were reduced over time.

Cognitio. "Investigation." A name conventionally given to a procedure in which a magistrate looked into a legal matter (potentially civil or criminal) and rendered a decision. Contrast the procedures of the *quaestiones* or formulary trials, in which the parties took the initiative and the case was decided only by the judge(s), who was himself not a government agent. *Cognitio* arose in the provinces, but under the Empire became the ordinary form of procedure in Rome as well.

Damnum infectum. "Damage not (yet) done." If a neighbor's property threatened yours (whether through construction, disrepair, or some other problem), you could get the praetor to force him to promise payment for the potential future damage.

Damnum iniuria datum. "Damage wrongly done." An early statute (the *lex Aquilia*) allowed you to collect compensation (doubled in some cases) for damage done to your property under certain circumstances. *See* Chapter 18 for details.

Delict. An offense against a person (not the whole community) that arises from general obligations rather than from a specific agreement. Delicts (such as accidental damage to property, defamation, and theft) form a middle category between purely civil actions (e.g., contracts, inheritance) and "public" criminal ones (e.g., treason, riot, forgery). *See* Chapter 18.

Digest. An enormous collection of the writings of earlier jurists, cut-and-pasted together by a team of editors at the direction of the emperor Justinian in the 530's AD. This is now our principal source for Roman law.

Edict. An order of a Roman magistrate. Some of these were ad hoc and temporary, others were standardized and reissued by the new magistrates in each succeeding year. The most important of these was the edict of the urban praetor ("the Edict"), which served as the basis for much of Roman civil law.

Emancipation. The freeing of a slave or child from the control of his or her owner/father.

Emptio venditio. Literally, "buying selling." The form of contract that governed sales.

Fideicomissum. A "trust" created by a will. Property was formally left to one person along with instructions to use it for a particular purpose, normally to pass it on to another person. The enforceability of a *fideicomissum*, especially to evade various normal rules of inheritance, varied considerably over time.

Filius familias. "Son of a family." A son of a living father, no matter what his age. (Also *filia familias*, a similarly situated daughter). Such a person had essentially no private law rights; the father owned all property and could impose punishments more or less at will.

Formula. An official instruction from the praetor to the judge hearing a particular case. It spelled out who the parties were, what the issues were, and what range of decisions could be handed down by the judge. Most formulas were pieced together from highly standardized language.

Freedman. A former slave. If freed by a Roman citizen in correct form, the freedman was himself a Roman citizen, though he had a few civic disadvantages and lingering responsibilities to his former owner (now "patron").

Guardian. Latin *tutor.* A man appointed to look out for the financial affairs of another. Children *sui iuris* had a guardian who managed their property until they came of age and was expected to act in their interests. Adult women had guardians who could only veto certain transactions, and could act in the family's or their own interests.

Heir. The person or persons who took over the property and obligations of a dead person. A will had to name at least one heir in order to be valid. In the absence of a will, the automatic rules of intestate succession did nothing but choose an heir (or several co-heirs). An heir is different from someone who received the gift of a specific amount of property in a will (called a "legacy").

In iure. "At law." The first phase of a formulary trial, in which the parties laid out their general positions to the praetor. If he felt the issue was appropriate for trial, he would then issue a formula naming a judge to hear the actual evidence and telling him what to decide. *See also apud iudicem.*

In potestate. "In power." Anyone with a living father (or paternal grandfather) was in the "power" of that ancestor.

Note that adult children are still under this power, but wives are not.

Infamia. A state of formal disgrace, accompanied by a variety of disabilities (inability to hold office, make certain pleadings in court, testify). Conviction of various crimes and delicts, defeat in civil trials on certain matters, and membership in certain professions all brought about various kinds of *infamia*.

Iniuria. "Wrong action." Harm to a free person's reputation (but not body) could result in an action in court resulting in the award of double (or more) damages. *See also damnum iniuria datum.*

Interdict. Any of several orders from the praetor commanding or forbidding certain actions, ordinarily at the request of another party. These were framed in effectively conditional form, so a target who ignored the order would typically have a chance to explain himself in court later.

Intestate. Without a (valid) will.

Iudex. A "judge" who decided civil cases or one of several "jurors" who heard criminal cases. The *iudex* was not an active presiding officer in either kind of procedure (in contrast to a modern judge).

Ius civile. "Law among citizens," a phrase often used to denote statute law (as opposed to the Edict) or to distinguish specifically Roman law from principles that spanned systems (called *ius gentium*).

Jurist. A specialist in legal matters. Jurists might give legal advice, write on legal matters, teach law, and/or (under the empire) be employed by the state as part of the legal apparatus. You did not have to be a jurist to argue cases in court; the more relevant skill there was public speaking.

Latin. In legal terms, this is a citizenship status giving some but not all of the rights of true Roman citizens. It comes from different sources at different periods.

Legacy. *See* "heir."

Legis actio. "Action at law." An early device of civil procedure. To bring a case to court you had to find and use the specific wording relevant to your cause of action. Later replaced by the formula system.

Locatio conductio. "Leasing hiring." The form of contract that governed leasing and hiring – for example, renting a building or hiring a person to perform a job.

Magistrate. An elected executive officer of the Roman government. They served one-year terms. There were several positions; they were ranked; and at each level there was a panel of officials rather than a single person.

Pater familias. "Father of a family." A male with no living ancestor in the male line. You did not actually have to have any children to be a *pater familias*. Also the "prudence of a good *pater familias*" is the standard of care demanded by the law in situations in which you are to take as good care of someone else's property as your own.

Patria potestas. "Fatherly power." The power of a *pater familias* over his children (and his sons' children). *See filius familias.*

Patron. *See* "freedman."

Peculium. Property controlled by slave or child *in potestate*, though technically still owned by the owner/father. Property could be added to or taken from the *peculium* at the discretion of the legal owner, but while it was there third parties could sue him to enforce agreements made by the slave/child.

Peregrine. A free person who was not a Roman citizen.

Pledge. A contract designed to give security for some debt or other obligation. The creditor received possession (but not ownership or even use) of the pledged property.

Pontiff. A type of Roman "priest," whose major responsibilities involved the interpretation of divine law as it related to property and the performance of religious ceremonies.

Praetor. The second-highest of the Roman magistrates (*see* above). They came to control much of the workings of the legal system. The "city" or "urban praetor" (chosen among those elected by lot) was particularly important in this respect as he was responsible for the Edict.

Quaestio. "Inquiry." The various procedures for prosecution of criminal offenses under the Republic, especially the standing jury courts of the end of that period.

Real. "Connected to a thing." Thus, a "real" contract is operative only once something has changed hands, and a "real" right (over some property) is valid anywhere, not just against a particular person. For instance, if you own a car (a real right), you can sue anyone for its return; if you rent it (not a real right), you can take direct action only against the rental agency whose responsibility it is to provide you with the vehicle.

Res (nec) mancipi. Roman property fell into two categories depending on whether it needed certain formal rituals to transfer its ownership or not (*nec* is used in the latter case). *Res mancipi* included slaves, land, and certain farm animals.

Restitutio in integrum. An order issued by the praetor to undo an earlier transaction – for instance, one in which a young person has been taken advantage of.

Senate. A body of senior aristocrats that met to advise the kings and later the consuls. The Senate had no authority to pass laws or issue edicts, but was highly influential with those who did have legal power.

Servitude. The right of one property owner to make (limited) use of an adjacent property – for instance, to draw water or just to pass through. *See* Chapter 14.

Societas. "Partnership." A contract that made the partners in some business venture liable to each other for the profits and expenses of that venture.

Statute. A law, usually permanent and of general validity, passed by the main lawmaking organ of a government (say, a modern city council or parliament or the Roman assemblies or emperor).

Stricti iuris. "According to strict law." The standard for judging cases involving a number of legal situations, including *stipulatio*. This involved a literal reading of any agreement and so was, among other things, an all-or-nothing affair.

Stipulatio. A contract in the form of an oral question and answer (using certain special words). Any legal subject matter could be covered. The true *stipulatio* was restricted to Roman citizens, but eventually parallel forms were created for more general use.

Sui iuris. "Of one's own right." Said of a person not under the power of a *pater familias*, whether because the *pater* is dead or because the son/daughter has been emancipated. (Thus any *pater familias* is *sui iuris*, but not the other way around; a woman can be *sui iuris* as well.)

Testatio. A written affidavit presented to a court instead of, or in addition to, oral testimony.

Title. Another term for ownership, sometimes used generally, sometimes to contrast title with more specific rights that could be redistributed. For instance, a modern landlord has title to his buildings, even if his rights to enter or modify them are limited. The Latin equivalent is *dominium*.

Usucapio. Acquisition of title by holding onto a piece of property for a set period of time with good justification. This is relevant only in the case of *res mancipi* that have been sold or given away, but without the formal ritual technically required to transfer ownership.

Usufruct. The right to use a property and collect profits derived from it. One has to be given usufruct by the owner of the property, typically as a legacy in a will. The title remains separate, and all rights revert to the owner when the holder of the usufruct dies.

Vindicatio. An action to claim ownership of a piece of property.

FURTHER READING

PRIMARY TEXTS

By far the most important source is the *Digest*.

> *There is an English translation by a team of scholars headed by Alan Watson; it comes as a stand-alone edition with a facing Latin original. At present there is no online English translation of the entire Digest.*

Watson, Alan (ed.) (1998). *The Digest of Justinian*. Philadelphia: University of Pennsylvania Press. [English]

———— (1985). *The Digest of Justinian*. Philadelphia: University of Pennsylvania Press. [English and Latin]

> *The titles of the* Digest *on the major delicts (theft,* iniuria, *and* damnum iniuria datum*) are easily accessible in a Penguin edition.*

Kolbert, C. (tr.) (1979). *The Digest of Roman law: Theft, Rapine, Damage and Insult*. New York: Penguin.

> *There is a very convenient edition of Gaius's* Institutes, *in both Latin and English, with notes and a generous outline.*

Robinson, O., and **Gordon, W.** (eds.) (1988). *The Institutes of Gaius*. Ithaca, N.Y.: Cornell University Press.

> *There is an edition, translation, and commentary on surviving statute law (of which there is surprisingly little) by another team.*

Crawford, M. (ed.) (1996). *Roman Statutes*. Bulletin of the Institute of Classical Studies, Supplement 64.

MODERN SCHOLARSHIP

Here I give a brief list of books for further reading. This is hardly a complete bibliography. Rather, it is meant to be a selection of works that may be useful and reasonably accessible on specific topics. The scholarly literature on Roman law presents a number of difficulties. Much of it is in foreign languages, and the English-language works often assume a knowledge of Latin or of modern scholarly languages. Even where there are no language problems, scholars may assume considerable knowledge of Roman legal detail, prior scholarship on Roman law, or sophisticated concepts of legal studies more generally. One result of this is that some important topics (e.g., contracts) will not be represented by monographs listed here. In these cases, however, there are enough general works listed (e.g., those of Borkowski, Johnston, and Nicholas) to provide some guidance.

Alexander, Michael (1990). *Trials in the Late Roman Republic, 149 BC to 50 BC*. Toronto: University of Toronto Press.
Brief listings for every known trial (civil and criminal) during the period given. Alexander lists the parties involved, the legal issues, the result, the sources, and other information.

Berger, Adolf (1991). *Encyclopedic Dictionary of Roman Law*. Philadelphia: American Philosophical Society.

Very handy reference work for the (Latin) terminology of Roman law.

Buckland, W. W. (1969). *The Roman Law of Slavery: The Condition of the Slave in Private Law from Augustus to Justinian.* New York: AMS Press.

Originally published in 1908, but still a handy compendium on this very important topic.

Borkowski, J. A. (2005). *Textbook on Roman Law.* Oxford and New York: Oxford University Press.

Crook, J. A. (1967). *Law and Life of Rome.* London: Thames & Hudson.

A very broad introduction to Roman law with much attention to social context and practical use of the law.

———— (1995). *Legal Advocacy in the Roman World.* London: Duckworth.

Particularly valuable for bringing together Egyptian documentary evidence for the practice of advocates in day-to-day litigation.

Frier, B. (1985). *The Rise of the Roman Jurists: Studies in Cicero's Pro Caecina* (Princeton, N.J.: Princeton University Press.

Written around a particular case of Cicero's, this book nonetheless looks into much broader issues of the status of jurists and their evolving role in the Roman legal system.

———— (1989). *A Casebook on the Roman Law of Delict.* Atlanta, Ga.: Scholars Press.

Collected texts (mostly drawn from the Digest*) laying out particular cases, with annotation, to explain a variety of concepts of the* *law of delict. This is the method by which American law schools generally teach.*

——— and **McGinn, Thomas** (2004). *A Casebook on Roman Family Law.* Oxford and New York: Oxford University Press.

Like the previous work, but covering family law.

Gardner, Jane F. (1986). *Women in Roman Law and Society.* London: Croom Helm.

——— (1998). *Family and Familia in Roman Law and Life.* New York: Clarendon Press.

These works focus on adoption, emancipation, and the relationship between mothers and their children.

Grubbs, Judith Evans (1995). *Law and Family in Late Antiquity: The Emperor Constantine's Marriage Legislation.* Oxford and New York: Clarendon Press, Oxford University Press.

——— (2002). *Women and the Law in the Roman Empire: A Sourcebook on Marriage, Divorce and Widowhood.* London and New York: Routledge.

Johnston, David (1988). *The Roman Law of Trusts.* Oxford: Clarendon Press.

*The history and use of trusts (*fideicommissa*) in the law of inheritance.*

——— (1999). *Roman Law in Context.* Cambridge and New York: Cambridge University Press.

A general introduction to Roman private law, with a special focus on its practical business applications.

Nicholas, Barry (1962). *An Introduction to Roman Law.* Oxford: Clarendon Press.

General introduction to Roman law from a modern lawyer's point of view.

Nippel, Wilfried (1995). *Public Order in Ancient Rome.* Cambridge and New York: Cambridge University Press.

Policing and other means to maintain public order.

Riggsby, Andrew M. (1999). *Crime and Community in Ciceronian Rome.* Austin, Tex.: University of Texas Press.

The procedures and offenses covered by the criminal courts of the late Republic.

Robinson, O. F. (1997). *The Sources of Roman Law: Problems and Methods for Ancient Historians.* London and New York: Routledge.

Detailed but readable account of both the sources for and sources of Roman law treated in Chapters 4 and 5 of this book.

Saller, Richard P. (1994). *Patriarchy, Property, and Death in the Roman Family.* Cambridge and New York: Cambridge University Press.

Sets out the legal rules for paternal authority in cultural and demographic context.

Tellegen-Couperus, O. E. (1993). *A Short History of Roman Law.* London and New York: Routledge.

A history not so much of the law as of legal (and related political) institutions.

Watson, Alan (1995). *The Spirit of Roman Law.* Athens: University of Georgia Press.

Watson has written an enormous quantity of very technical works on all areas of the law, but this is a very basic account of his theories on the general production and interpretation of the law.

INDEX

✿✿✿✿✿✿✿✿

patron, 102, 177
peculium, 109, 245
penalties, 170–1, 189–90, 191, 192,
    198–9, 202–3, 224, 250
personality principle, 103, 215–17, 257
pledge, *see* contract(s)
Pliny (the younger), 36, 60–1, 262–3
pontiff, 52, 205, 210, 213, 259, 263
possession, 139–42
praetor, *see* magistrate(s)
Proculians, 60
prosecution, 51, 75
prostitution, 72, 74, 180, 203
publicans, 132

quaestio (criminal court), 197–8

real rights, 146
res (nec) mancipi, 137, 168
rescripts, 90
responses, 27, 28, 90
restitutio in integrum, 30, 108
rhetoric, 3–4, 48, 51, 58, 61, 95
risk, 126–7, 130–1, 246, 251

Sabinians, 60–1
sacred things, 206–8, 224, 257–9, 263
sale, *see* contract(s)
security, 80, 108, 150, 168, 244, 247
Senate, 12–13, 15, 18–19, 26–7, 62, 105,
    197, 200, 203, 207, 209, 210–11
  senatus consultum Orphitianum, 161
  senatus consultum Tertullianum, 161
servitude(s), 146–9, 260

Servius Sulpicius Rufus, 3, 49
shame, 68, 72–5, 180, 199
slaves, 62, 68–9, 99–103, 105, 108–9,
    180, 188, 192, 193, 203, 236, 241,
    242
social control, 189–90
societas, *see* contract(s)
statute, 26–7, 30–1, 216
stipulatio, *see* contract(s)
stricti iuris, 123–5
sui iuris, 107, 166

tablets, wax, 41–2, 97, 235, 252
television, 44, 231
testatio, 95–6
texbooks, 38–9, 61, 64
theft, *see* delict(s)
tirocinium fori, 58–9, 63
title, 125
Twelve Tables, 26, 48, 59, 88, 159, 191

usucapio, 138–9, 142
usufruct, 143–6, 148
usus, *see* usufruct

vindicatio, 138, 139, 141–2
violence, 68–70, 140, 200–1

weapons, 44, 68–9, 203
wills, 91, 102, 104, 154–7, 239, 254, 255
  "undutiful," 156
witnesses, 80–1, 84, 115, 198, 200
women, 57, 74, 81, 155, 165–71, 177, 193,
    252; *see also* gender

23511838R00186

Made in the USA
Middletown, DE
26 August 2015